THE
DARLINGTON
SPITFIRE

THE DARLINGTON SPITFIRE

A charmed life

PETER CAYGILL

Airlife
England

Copyright © 1999 Peter Caygill

First published in the UK in 1999
by Airlife Publishing Ltd

British Library Cataloguing-in-Publication Data
A catalogue record for this book
is available from the British Library

ISBN 1 84037 076 9

The information in this book is true and complete to the best our knowledge. All
recommendations are made without any guarantee on the part of the Publisher, who
also disclaims any liability incurred in connection with the use of this data or specific
details.

Typeset by Servis Filmsetting Ltd, Manchester
Printed in England by St Edmundsbury Press Ltd, Bury St Edmunds, Suffolk

Airlife Publishing Ltd
101 Longden Road, Shrewsbury, SY3 9EB, England

Acknowledgements

Thanks to the enthusiastic support received from individuals and organisations, a small research project which was set in motion two years ago has evolved into this book.

I would like to thank all former pilots of the Darlington Spitfire who have given up precious time to reply to my enquiries; in particular Ted Andrews, Tony Bruce, Tony Cooper, Peter Dunning, Stan Farmiloe, Gordon Farquharson, David Ferraby, Roy Flight, Stan Halloran, 'Paddy' Harbison, Scott Morrison, Ray Stebbings and Ian Walker.

In addition, many other Spitfire pilots have provided useful information – my sincere thanks go to Walter Johnston for providing much background detail, and to Neville Duke, Norman Edwards, the late 'Laddie' Lucas, James Pickering, Tony Smith, Sid 'Watty' Watson and 'Bertie' Wootten for their memories and help in tracing former squadron colleagues.

I have been most fortunate in contacting the families of several ex-pilots and I am deeply indebted to Patricia Kingaby for supplying copies of her father's logbook, together with extracts from his unpublished autobiography, to Peter May, for information relating to his father, and to Mrs Margaret Grigor for help regarding her brother Ian Duncan.

Considerable assistance has also been provided by other aviation researchers and my thanks in particular go to Martin Johnston and Roy Nixon.

Finally, I have been helped by many organisations and I would like to acknowledge the co-operation received from the staff at Darlington Library, Public Record Office, Imperial War Museum, RAF Museum, Air Historical Branch of the MoD, National Railway Museum, Darlington Museum.

For Mum

Introduction

Most people, even those with little aviation knowledge, when asked to name three types of aircraft, would probably include the Supermarine Spitfire. Although a relatively modern creation, it has already become part of a legend that would have us believe that it was this country's saviour in the Battle of Britain.

In the dark days of 1940, after the humiliation of Dunkirk, the British Nation needed proof of its technical excellence, and there was a deep desire to find a weapon of war that would stop the Germans in their tracks. The doctrine of aerial bombardment had been widely expounded in the 1930s and the *Luftwaffe* had used it to devastating effect in their invasion of Western Europe. Britain could only anticipate more of the same, so it was natural for its people to look to the RAF's Fighter Command for their salvation. Already blessed with an aura of glamour, the exigencies of war boosted the Spitfire's reputation to almost mythical proportions, the mixture of fact and fiction which enhanced its stature having been the source of constant debate ever since.

The Spitfire was able to cope with considerable development, and it easily accepted more powerful engines and heavier armament which kept it in the forefront of fighter technology until the end of World War Two. The subject of this book entered service in July 1941 by which time Fighter Command had moved from defence to attack with its first forays into occupied Europe. By the time of its demise, the Allied air offensive had multiplied to such proportions as to be irresistible, and victory was tantalisingly close. Unlike most other long serving Spitfires of its generation, this Spitfire flew only with operational squadrons, never with second line units, and eventually amassed over 200 sorties, a prodigious figure considering that the vast majority of its time was spent in the hazardous skies over northern France, Holland and Belgium.

This is the story not only of an aircraft which played a significant part in Royal Air Force history, but of many of the pilots who flew it during its long and illustrious career. Generally in their early twenties, though sometimes younger, they came from all parts of the free world to fight the same cause and share the stresses and strains which are inherent in combat flying. To the thrill of flying one of the all-time classic fighter aircraft and the camaraderie generated among a close knit team, was added the sorrow brought about by the inevitable losses, or as one of its pilots put it, 'The fun and the grief'.

The beginning of the account lies not in the aircraft's entry into service however, but in the County Durham town of Darlington whose people raised the necessary money so that a Mark Vb could be called *The Darlington Spitfire*.

Contents

Chapter 1	**Spitfire fever**	9
Chapter 2	**Biggin on the bump**	18
Chapter 3	**Gravesend**	31
Chapter 4	**Castletown**	43
Chapter 5	**Back in the fray**	50
Chapter 6	**Coltishall**	66
Chapter 7	**Deanland**	80
Chapter 8	**Predannack**	97
Chapter 9	**200 Not out**	108
Chapter 10	**Finger trouble**	117
Chapter 11	**The Pilots**	121

Appendices
A	**Squadrons and Bases**	154
B	**Combat Claims**	155
C	**Pilots**	156
D	**Operations Log**	158
E	**Non-operational Flying**	164
F	**North Star**	166

| Bibliography | 168 |
| Index | 169 |

Chapter One

Spitfire fever

Of all the fund-raising activities intended to assist the war effort during the Second World War, one of the most popular was the 'Spitfire Fund' and throughout Britain and the Empire well over £7 million was raised which resulted in the naming of approximately 1500 Spitfires. The presentation of aircraft was not a new idea and had also taken place during the First World War when over 500 aircraft of a wide variety of types carried their donors' inscriptions during service with the Royal Flying Corps and the Royal Naval Air Service. One notable difference between the two wars was the public's identification in the second conflict with one particular type of aircraft – the Spitfire. Created by the great R.J. Mitchell, designer of Supermarine's Schneider racers of a decade earlier, the Spitfire possessed a grace of line which, together with its state-of-the-art performance, led to the development of a mystique that has survived to this day.

This fascination with the Spitfire produced a situation that was extremely unfair to the Hawker Hurricane. Devotees of Camm's workhorse would argue that it destroyed more enemy aircraft during the Battle of Britain than all other forms of defence put together, but even they were unable to deny that it just did not look as good! A few Hurricanes were named, but this was usually due to the donors failing to specify that they wanted a Spitfire. With the public's willingness to donate, all that was needed was to ascertain the cost of a Spitfire. This was fixed at £5000, the equivalent of £135,000 at today's prices. Although this was very much a nominal figure which did not reflect the true cost, as private donations were merely added to public funding it was accurate enough.

Fund-raising activities tended to reflect the general war situation, and little was actually achieved until after the German *Blitzkrieg* into France in 1940. With the beginning of the Battle of Britain, Spitfire Funds were set up in ever-increasing numbers and the people of Darlington began to call for their own fund to be formed. As further incentive, the Battle of Britain came to the North East on 15 August when sixty-five Heinkel He 111s of KG 26, escorted by thirty-four Messerschmitt Me 110s of ZG 76, flew from their bases in Norway in an attempt to raid a number of northern airfields. The *Luftwaffe* had assumed that all of Fighter Command's reserves had been committed to the battle in the south, so it came as an unpleasant surprise to encounter stiff opposition which broke up the attack and accounted for eight bombers and seven fighters shot down, including an Me 110 which crashed at Streatlam near Barnard Castle.

Fund-raising in Darlington actually commenced in August, even before official sanction was granted from the Town's Corporation for the creation of a scheme. Some of the first to contribute were the girls of Peases Mill, who offered to have 3d deducted from their pay each week, and the skaters of South Park who organised a fancy dress carnival with all proceeds going to the fund. Official blessing was not long in coming however, and the *Northern Despatch* of 3 September carried a general notice from the Mayor, Councillor John Dougill, announcing the appeal to raise £5000 for a Spitfire, together with a further appeal for 2000 guineas for an X-Ray ambulance.

Another early contributor was Mr S. Newton, licensee of the Greyhound Hotel in Parkgate, who decided to give a ha'penny for every German aircraft brought down over the UK. As he was reliant on the official figures published in the press, which for the period 18–31 August alone stood at 534, Mr. Newton ended up donating a considerable sum. It was not generally appreciated until after the war that defence claims were greatly overestimated, a situation which had the effect of boosting morale, and one that also led to Darlington's Spitfire Fund being a fortunate beneficiary.

A major contributor to the fund was Darlington's Civil Defence Force which was made up of the Air Raid Precautions Organisation and the Auxiliary Fire Service. One hundred and fifty pounds had been accumulated by the time the scheme was announced, and eventually over £1000 was raised by weekly deductions and various fund-raising activities. One enterprising ARP warden had gained temporary possession of a German incendiary bomb and proceeded to raise £2. 12s by giving lectures on its construction, and how to deal with it.

The first of what was to be a regular feature appeared in the *Northern Despatch* on 4 September giving details of fund-raising activities, and reminding everyone where to send donations. Under the title 'Spitfire Corner', every contribution, however small, was given credit, and several of the more meritorious efforts were singled out for closer analysis. Thanks to everyone's efforts, the total soon began to rise, and by the end of September it was already £1700.

On 20 September, the Mayor announced the receipt of a gift of

Spitfire fever

One of the early 'Spitfire Corner' articles which kept the people of Darlington up to date with the town's fund-raising activities. (Northern Echo)

NORTHERN DESPATCH, FRIDAY, 20 SEPTEMBER, 1940

SPITFIRE CORNER

THREE DARLINGTON BOYS RAISE £14

A grand effort by three small boys, all under 11 years of age, has resulted in £14 1s being handed over to the Spitfire Fund. They are Dicky Wilson, Stanley Bowran and Ronnie Gent, all of Eastbourne-road. These three youngsters held jumble sales in Eastbourne-road after collecting all kinds of gifts from friends and neighbours and just how hard they must have worked is reflected in the final result.

There is nothing like a little friendly rivalry to help on an effort. Kitty Urwin, of 44, Bensham-road, with the help of her friends, Joan Elliott, of 47, Bensham-road, and Pauline Birkett, of 45, Bensham-road, decided to

MAYOR OF DARLINGTON'S FUNDS

Contributions to the Mayor's Funds can be sent to the following:—

SPITFIRE FUND
Mr. C. W. Burnip,
Hon. Treasurer,
Barclays Bank, High Row,
Darlington.
Northern Despatch Office,
Priestgate, Darlington.

X-RAY AMBULANCE
Mr. Trevor Morris,
Hon. Treasurer,
Midland Bank, Ltd.,
Darlington.

or donations may be paid direct to any of the banks in the town.

run an effort themselves after Kitty's brother and his pals had raised 12s 6d for the Fund. The girls held little efforts among their friends and their delight knew no bounds when they found that they had raised £1 1s, and beaten the boys by 8s 6d.

A JUMBLE SALE

A jumble sale organised by Vera Johnson, of 36, Grasmere-road, and Doreen Ripley, of 38, Grasmere-road, raised £3 10s. Robert Young, of 53, Lansdowne-street, Terence Keelan, of 9,

Lansdowne-street, and John Glancy, of 64, Lansdowne-street, brought in £2 2s, being money they had raised from the sale of gifts collected from friends.

Another sale arranged by Pauline Collier, Edith Ridley and Molly Reed, all of Maude-street, realised £1 3s 6d.

A Spitfire Bazaar organised by Jean and Enid Wright, of 207, Longfield-road, Kitty and Ernest Scott, 147, Crosby-street, and Dorothy Eltringham, of 7, Brian-road, was a big success. The children raised £2 6s by this effort.

Iris Hall, of 40, Thompson-street West, held a "lone effort," and her contribution to the Spitfire Fund was £2.

THIRD SUBSCRIPTION

Another subscription — the third—has been received from No. 7 Bay and Others, Robert Stephenson and Hawthorn's, Ltd., per T.C., A.L., J.W. This week's donation was £1.

The caretaker at Messrs. Summerson and Sons, Ltd., Albert-road, raised by efforts the sum of £3.

A whist drive held at 33, Brinkburn-road, the home of Mrs. Lund, of 35, Brinkburn-road, resulted in the sum of £2 2s being handed over to the fund. There were no expenses in connection with this effort, prizes and refreshments being given. Mrs. Rhymer and Mrs. Lund now intend holding another whist drive for the X-ray Ambulance Fund.

HAWES BOY HELPS SPITFIRE FUND

A little boy living at Hawes has set a fine example of unselfishness in connection with Wensleydale's effort to raise money for a Spitfire. He went into a shop in Hawes with a penny in his hand and asked for a penny packet of chewing gum. While he was being served he noticed a Wensleydale Spitfire collecting box on the counter, so he changed his mind, remarking "Nay, I'll not bother about t' chewing gum. I'll give mi penny to t' Spitfire Fund instead."

although they had lived locally before the war at Haughton Hall and Dinsdale Manor respectively. Although the money was to be kept separate from that being raised in Darlington, the Mayor expressed his hope that such a generous donation would provide a stimulus to the town's own efforts. The two cheques were passed directly to the Ministry of Aircraft Production and eventually led to the naming of Spitfire, AD387 *North Star* (see Appendix F).

At around the same time another Spitfire Fund was launched in Darlington, one that came about as a result of the jealousy of a young girl. Eight-year-old Dorothy Lofthouse of West House, Elton Parade, was delighted to discover that a Spitfire was to fly which carried her name. A Mrs Dorothy Clark from London had raised the necessary £5000 and this led to the naming of Mark Vb AB201 as *Dorothy of Great Britain and the Empire*. Dorothy's ten-year-old sister Pat felt rather left out by all of this and was made to suffer accordingly for not having a Spitfire named after her. When her father, Major G.A. Lofthouse of the Green Howards, returned home on leave, she attempted to persuade him to launch a 'Pat' fund to even things up. Major Lofthouse could see that family harmony was at risk, so he agreed to the proposal and asked for contributions from all 'Pats', including Patricks, Patricias and Patiences, beginning with some famous Pats of the day, Patsy Hendren, the cricketer, and the actress Pat Kirkwood. Although the records relating to presentation aircraft are incomplete, it would appear that this particular fund did not achieve the required total and, sadly, it seems that Pat Lofthouse did not see a Spitfire carry her name into the air.

In the meantime the appeal for money for the town's Spitfire had been taken up by some of the villages surrounding Darlington. The residents of Great Stainton and Bishopton together raised £38. 10s. 7d and the fund was swelled further with the receipt of £7. 10s from the Gainford Horticultural Society, £100 from Croft Young Farmers club, and £12. 5s from the proceeds of a Spitfire Dance held in Heighington.

As well as the generosity of ordinary people, many of Darlington's industrial concerns and businesses also made contributions including Whessoe Foundry, Darlington Rolling Mills, Thomas Summersons and the Chemical Insulating Co., who all provided £100. One of the most impressive collecting performances was that of Darlington's butchers who together raised just over £250. This figure included £50 from various members of the Zissler family, a business that is still going strong after more than 125 years.

The Spitfire Fund inspired many of Darlington's children to raise

Spitfire fever

A novel mirror collection at the George Hotel, Darlington, in aid of the Spitfire Fund. There is almost £50 on it.—[N.D.]

Spitfire mirror at the George Hotel, Darlington, which raised just over £38.
(Northern Echo)

money and their efforts from start to finish provided the unique character of the town's appeal. Back streets proved to be the ideal location for auctions and jumble sales, and the community spirit of the times ensured that these events were a huge success. The youngsters were rewarded by reports of their efforts appearing in 'Spitfire Corner', often accompanied by their photographs. Although the individual amounts raised were generally small, collectively they formed a considerable sum which would be instrumental in the town achieving its target.

The rivalry between groups of friends, and between boys and girls, was often intense as each tried to outdo the other in the amount of money that they could raise. There were to be many tense moments in the offices of the *Northern Despatch* as eager youngsters watched their sealed containers being prised open and the contents counted, agonisingly slowly.

Some children had personal reasons for contributing to the fund, while others responded to events elsewhere. Rosemary Iannarelli felt that something had to be done as her father had been taken as a prisoner-of-war and she was desperate for him to be back home again. Reasoning that the best way to achieve this was by helping the war effort, she organised a jumble sale at her home in Falmer Street which raised over £5.

A jumble sale organised by John Trotter and James Martin of Olympic Street came about after news that a ship carrying children to Canada, to escape the bombing, had been sunk by a U-Boat, and that many had died. The sale was held in John's backyard which was brightly decorated for the occasion with bunting and flags. The family air raid shelter, which was also suitably adorned, was put to good use with the hard working youngsters being treated to jelly and custard. Although the boys, who were both nine years old, had collected what Mrs Trotter could only describe as 'junk', she was delighted, and also somewhat amazed, when everything was sold.

In addition to organising events, many children made individual efforts, including eight-year-old Nina Clennell from the Railway Hotel, Hopetown, who sold her rocking horse for £3. 10s. 6d and made two other contributions to raise over £7 in total. Billy Bean of Woodvale Road donated his pocket money of 1s., Mavis Goodger of Dale Road raised £1 through selling pin cushions, kettle holders and dolls clothes that she had made herself, and Roy Woodman made use of German propaganda leaflets by selling them to raise 6s.

By now the country was gripped by 'Spitfire fever' and in recent weeks literally hundreds of Spitfire Funds had been set up throughout the length and breadth of Great Britain. Amongst all this fund-raising activity nationwide, Darlington's own appeal may well have been unique in that it received a contribution from a dog! An Airedale Terrier by the name of Ruff, who lived with his owners in Merrybent, celebrated his fourteenth birthday in October by donating a guinea. This happy occasion was marked by Ruff's photograph appearing in 'Spitfire Corner' together with those of other fund raisers.

By the end of October the total raised had reached £3700 but this did not impress vice-president of the Chamber of Trade, Mr O.W. White, who thought it 'deplorable' that the target should still be some way off and that it was a 'slur on Darlington'. Other voices on the committee were more moderate and in comparison with many towns, Darlington was putting up a creditable performance. Throughout the duration of the fund, the Chamber of Trade formed what might be termed a 'think

Spitfire fever

usy as any r answered, us. One of day had a e went into wn to do came back e his shop-

losing day,' oked at the ered it was

ARMED

drama lies l of The Boy Gilt Cross ul Kaye, a th Shanghai d assassin e house two aye's home upant, Mr. Kaye heard ams of the immediately e. He suc g with the n threw him vn the road. and again t during the ice, who was earby, fired hip, and he in his hold. Municipal nting Kaye rist watch in his gallant t if others e spirit their easier.

ad preached r on The w," he said, kuk. Where

seat," said a awa' hame."

RK DID

e since 1903 s were fired f the 12-inch rown of the t defences on f Long Island

Capt. Honeyman, to be held on 15 December

The goal is now in sight, but this does not mean that there should be a slackening of effort. One final spurt by the town would see the £5,000 reached and probably passed.

Mavis Goodger, of 37, Daleroad, who, by the way, celebrates her birthday to-day, raised £1 for the Fund by making pin cushions, kettleholders, doll's clothes, etc., and selling them among friends and neighbours.

MAVIS GOODGER. Mavis did not believe in having a stall and waiting until people came to buy, she took her goods to her friends and made sure of her "sales."

Four boys from the Springfield district, Derek Richards, Donald Lawther, Frank Fenton, and James Smith, all of Locomotivestreet, held a jumble sale in the street and made £3. They collected anything that would sell from their neighbours, and were helped in their effort by Miss A. Lawther, also of Locomotivestreet.

A collection box brought in by Emily Armstrong and Margaret

Maurice Craig and Dorothy and George James, who raised £2 2s. from a jumble sale held in Locomotive-street.

Robson, both of Haughton-road, contained 4s 1d.

The 13th—and last—contribution of £1 16s from No. 7 Bay

mark whateve making Som when t shops i in the busines can sca pert su of our hundre Now the pro mises line o represe letters of thos only a In thos as nur busine

Quaint All styles designs painted conspic hatch catch Even Bardsle being s into a populac ments herself sufficie what w unicorr winged stop th had to The speciall engross they so recogni which connec have l Black Heads, and B

Specia Relic remain the er once 8 he was broker beater'

tank' to find new ways of generating money, although the schemes that they came up with varied considerably in their creativity. One member's imagination did not extend beyond offering to auction one of his sheep, but a colleague, Mr G.E. Redd, hit on an excellent idea which was the forerunner of today's charity shops. He proposed setting up a small shop where people could donate articles which could then be sold. The idea was given the go-ahead and for a period of two months, White's shop in Tubwell Row became the 'Spitfire Shop' which eventually raised over £90.

Commemorative plaque issued to Darlington by the MAP. (Author)

IN THE HOUR OF PÉRIL PEOPLE OF DARLINGTON EARNED THE GRATITUDE OF THE BRITISH NATIONS SUSTAINING THE VALOUR OF THE ROYAL AIR FORCE AND FORTIFYING THE CAUSE OF FREEDOM BY THE GIFT OF SPITFIRE AIRCRAFT

They shall mount up with wings as eagles

Issued by the Ministry of Aircraft Production
1941

A further £1000 was raised during November at the end of which Darlington held its War Weapons Week. Although it did not contribute to the Spitfire Fund, there were plenty of people willing to pay 6d. to see a Messerschmitt Me 109 which had been shot down near East Peckham in Kent on 2 October. This aircraft was a 109E-4, *Werke Nr* 5901, and had been flown by *Oberleutnant* Ludwig Fiel of II/JG 53 who had lost out in a battle with a 603 Squadron Spitfire. Having been paraded through the town, it was then exhibited at the Post Office exchange in Barnard Street, and gave everyone the opportunity to see what their own Spitfire would eventually be up against.

The £5000 mark was finally passed during the first week of January 1941, the cheque being presented to the new Mayor, Councillor H. Wilcock, by Mr C.W. Burnip, Treasurer of Barclays Bank. The actual amount raised was £5137. 16s. 2d., although £100 was transferred to the X-Ray Ambulance fund so that its target could be achieved at the same time. In his letter to the Ministry of Aircraft Production, the Mayor praised the efforts of the ARP and AFS, but special emphasis was given to the numerous children who had done so much to achieve the target. In return, a letter of appreciation was received from Lord Beaverbrook praising the 'Spirit of generous patriotism displayed by the people of Darlington'. Along with other towns and organisations who presented aircraft to the RAF, a small commemorative plaque was issued by the MAP. For many years this was displayed at the Darlington Museum in Tubwell Row but, following the museum's closure in April 1998, the plaque is now available for viewing at the town library in Crown Street.

Chapter Two

Biggin on the bump

The people of Darlington had to wait until 29 October 1941 to hear news of 'their' Spitfire when two photographs and a short description were published in the *Northern Despatch*. The report described the Spitfire as one of Britain's fastest and hardest-hitting machines, and it also informed readers that its latest Rolls-Royce Merlin engine propelled it to a speed approaching 400 mph. Even so, with the advent of the Focke-Wulf Fw 190A in the late summer of 1941, there were many Spitfire V pilots who felt that it didn't approach it quite close enough!

The Spitfire that was allocated to Darlington was Mark Vb W3320, one of a batch of 450 ordered on 22 February 1940, to contract 19713/39, and built by Vickers-Armstrongs (Supermarine) Ltd. The Mark V variant was to be produced in greater numbers than any other mark of Spitfire even though it was considered at the time to be very much of a stop-gap. The Mark III, with its two-stage supercharged Merlin XX, was initially envisaged to be the next-generation Spitfire, but its development was delayed due to problems with its Rolls-Royce engine. This situation was exacerbated because the Hurricane II, which also used the Merlin XX, was awarded priority of engine supply as it would otherwise have quickly become obsolescent.

At the end of 1940 it was considered that any future daylight attacks on Britain were likely to be by aircraft operating at much higher altitudes than previously encountered. At around this time Rolls-Royce developed the Merlin 45, which was similar to the Merlin XX but with the low-altitude blower deleted, thereby optimizing its performance at altitude. This engine closely matched the RAF's requirements as it promised to make the Spitfire much more effective at greater heights. As the new engine could be easily adapted to the Mark II airframe with the minimum amount of modification, the Spitfire III was effectively killed off. The Merlin 45 engined Spitfire became the Mark V, which was regarded as being a temporary measure pending development of the Mark VI with its pressure cabin and extended wingtips. As things turned out, the concern over high altitude attack proved to be unfounded and only 100 Mark VI Spitfires were eventually produced compared with 6479 of the 'interim' Mark V.

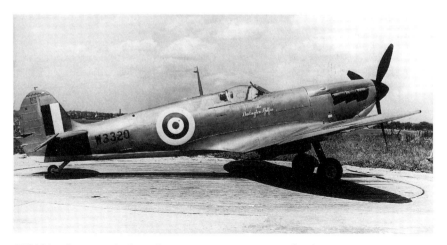

W3320, photographed on the compass swing at Eastleigh, June 1941.
(via Darlington Library)

Visually there was little to distinguish the Spitfire V from the earlier versions; apart from a slightly altered nose profile, the only other feature was a larger oil cooler under the port wing. The main difference lay in the Merlin 45 which was rated at 1440 hp, its improved supercharger allowing maximum boost pressure to be raised to +16 lb/sq.in. Although top speed was only marginally improved at 369 mph, the Mark V showed considerable improvement in rate of climb and service ceiling. Armament in the Mark Vb comprised two 20mm Hispano cannon, with 60 rounds per gun, and four 0.303-in. Browning machine-guns, each with 350 rounds.

Darlington's Spitfire was taken into the air for the first time on 11 June 1941, by Supermarine test pilot George Pickering from the factory airfield at Eastleigh. Everything worked perfectly and the next day it was delivered to No. 9 Maintenance Unit (MU) at Cosford to be fitted out with its operational equipment. On 12 July, after the completion of this work, it was flown to Biggin Hill where it joined 'B' Flight of 92 Squadron.

As one of Fighter Command's premier squadrons, 92 had earned a reputation second to none during the Battle of Britain, and had since gone on to account for more enemy aircraft destroyed than any other unit. The achievements of its pilots had been widely reported by the national press and as a result the names of Kingcome, Bartley, Wright and Kingaby were all well known by the public. By the summer of 1941 the composition of the squadron had begun to change, many of the old regulars had gone to be replaced by new pilots, including nineteen-year-old Pilot Officer Neville Duke, who after the war became Chief Test Pilot at Hawker Aircraft Ltd. Number 92 Squadron's Commanding Officer was Scotsman Squadron Leader Jamie Rankin DFC who, since his arrival in February, had rapidly built a reputation as one of Fighter Command's foremost fighting leaders.

If 92 was one of the RAF's best known squadrons, Biggin Hill was without doubt its most famous airfield. Situated on a plateau on the North Downs to the south of Bromley, Biggin had first been developed in 1917 by the Royal Flying Corps for wireless telegraphy experiments for which its elevated position proved to be ideal. Its proximity to London endowed upon it a strategic role in the defence of the capital, a fact which was not lost on the *Luftwaffe* which had raided the airfield heavily during the Battle of Britain. The scars were still evident a year later by which time Fighter Command had gone onto the offensive with operations over Northern France aimed at causing a high rate of attrition among the opposing fighter force, and preventing French based units transferring to the Russian Front. Biggin Hill's Wing Leader was the supreme fighter pilot and master tactician, Wing Commander A.G. 'Sailor' Malan DSO, DFC, who, in the two months prior to W3320's arrival, had destroyed thirteen enemy aircraft.

During its stay with 92 Squadron, whose radio call sign was 'Garrick', W3320 was heavily involved in fighter sweeps and 'Circuses' over France, together with occasional defensive patrols and convoy protection duties. When the weather precluded the use of larger formations, pairs of aircraft often operated on the so-called 'Rhubarb' sorties over France, looking for targets of opportunity and taking advantage of cloud cover to evade defensive fighters. Its main adversary in combat was the Messerschmitt Me109F and in performance there was little to choose between the two. With its lower wing-loading, the Spitfire had a clear advantage in the turn, but the 109 was superior in the vertical plane. As a consequence, the tactics employed by the *Luftwaffe* usually consisted of dive attacks followed either by a zoom climb to regain height initiative, or by continuing the dive to lower levels. Survival for Spitfire pilots thus depended on seeing the 109s early enough to be able to break into them. If the 109 could be lured into a one-to-one combat at similar speeds, the superior manoeuvrability of the Spitfire gave it the upper hand.

The Darlington Spitfire began its operational career in the evening of 20 July 1941 when it was flown on a Channel sweep by Flight Sergeant Don Kingaby, who was to be its regular pilot for the next three months.

Sergeant Don Kingaby DFM. (Imperial War Museum ref CH3555)

Although only twenty-one years of age, Kingaby was already a combat veteran and had run up an impressive tally of fourteen enemy aircraft destroyed. He was the son of the Reverend P.F. Kingaby, vicar at the village of Impington to the north of Cambridge, and following an education at King's School, Ely, he worked as a clerk in an insurance office during which time he joined the RAF Volunteer Reserve. Following call-up and flight training, his first posting was to 266 Squadron at Wittering, but it was not until he joined 92 Squadron on 25 September 1940 that his true abilities as a fighter pilot came to the fore. Inspired by the example of his new colleagues, his score quickly began to rise and his greatest day occurred on 15 November 1940, when he shot down four Me109s in the course of two sorties, an achievement that led to the immediate award of a Distinguished Flying Medal (DFM). His apparent predilection for disposing of the premier German fighter led to the press dubbing him 'the 109 specialist', and during the summer of 1941 he would enhance this reputation with his new aircraft.

Of medium build, and with a pleasant, easy going manner, Kingaby was far removed from the public's image of the dashing fighter pilot. Sergeant Walter 'Johnnie' Johnston, who came from Newcastle-upon-Tyne, arrived at Biggin just a few days before the Darlington Spitfire and recalls his first impressions:

> 'When I first saw him, I thought he was a line-shooter! "Hunk" Humphreys, Stan (Harrison) and myself had arrived from 152 in Cornwall to find the squadron away on a show. We went down to disper-

Sergeant Walter 'Johnnie' Johnston with a member of his groundcrew in front of W3314 QJ-H at Biggin Hill. (Johnston)

sal to meet the others and the groundstaff, and when the squadron arrived back, we three were in the crew room. The door burst open and a tousled, tired group came through with a little chap in front saying "Did you see all those *Stukas* on the deck at Calais Marck? Hell, if they are waiting for another bash over here it'll be grand. If I don't get eight or ten on the trip, I'll be disappointed!"

'All were in shirt sleeves so no ranks could be seen, but this little fellow seemed as if he was one of the ringleaders. Then he noticed three new faces and at once came over to us. When we introduced ourselves as the new replacements and said we already had about eight months with 152, he nearly fell on us and kissed us, calling out to the others that at last sense had prevailed. It was only then that he put on his jacket and I saw the DFM and Bar and I knew then that it wasn't conceit, just experience!'

After this uncertain start, Johnston and Kingaby became good friends and eventually decided to share a room together as both had suffered the loss of room-mates before they even had the chance to get to know them. Indeed, so many pilots fresh out of OTU had been lost within a matter of days, that 'Sailor' Malan had made repeated demands that all replacement pilots destined for the Biggin Hill Wing should have combat experience. Johnston and Kingaby each respected the other's flying ability, and they shared what Johnston describes as: 'a highly defined sense of self-preservation', so that if anyone was going to make it through, they would.

Back at dispersals, any keen observer would have noticed that W3320 was not the only Spitfire on 92 Squadron with a North East connection. There was also W3324 which carried the name *Newcastle-upon-Tyne II*. Don Kingaby did fly this particular aircraft but obviously preferred the Darlington example which, with the exception of one incident, was to serve him well for the rest of his time with the squadron. Although it was occasionally flown by other pilots, W3320 was very much Don Kingaby's own machine and he lost no time in having it painted up to his liking. As a Supermarine-built aircraft, the presentation title had been placed on the starboard side of the cockpit, so that squadron and personal markings adorned the port side. There was a German cross for each of his fourteen victories, and below these was Kingaby's own lion emblem. Forward of these markings it carried the title 'East India Squadron', as 92 had been named as a gift squadron following the donation of funds for the war effort. Sadly, no further markings were allowed, unlike a cartoon which appeared in the *Northern Despatch* and showed an aircraft with 'Buy It In Darlington' emblazoned under one wing, and 'Shops Open Every Bank Holiday Monday' on the other'!

Don Kingaby got to know his new aircraft well over the next few days as 92 Squadron maintained Fighter Command's policy of 'leaning forward' into France with two, and sometimes three, sweeps each day. The *Luftwaffe* did not always put in an appearance, but an evening operation on the 23rd produced a number of encounters, and Sergeant Geoff Hickman shot down an Me109 in flames. The following day saw the RAF in action over a wide front with heavy bomber attacks against the *Scharnhorst* and *Gneisenau* at La Pallice and Brest, together with raids by 2 Group Blenheims on Cherbourg. Number 11 Group squadrons gave assistance to their comrades from Bomber Command by operating intensively over north-eastern France which prevented the locally based fighters from taking any part in the actions further to the west. Number 92 Squadron flew two sweeps in quick succession, with Don Kingaby flying W3320 in the first before handing over to Pilot Officer Percy Beake for the second. Walter Johnston flew on both operations and recalls:

> 'The first trip was quiet with no immediate enemy reaction, just bags of twitch, but the second sweep made up for it. My logbook comments read:

Pilot Officer Percy Beake in W3459 Cape Town V, *the aircraft in which Flight Lieutenant 'Tommy' Lund was shot down on 2 October 1941.* (Imperial War Museum ref CH 4166)

"In at Dunkirk, then got engaged. Attacked by two, then three. Chased back by seven 109Fs. Landed Hornchurch with two gallons left." The action took place very high indeed and I was really hanging on my prop before we got mixed up. I claimed two 109Fs as probables ... and last saw them going into cloud at around 15,000 ft. "Sailor" Malan saw the 109s go down, on each occasion in a fairly tight spiral, not a spin, the first trailing white/grey smoke, the second likewise, turning black later. He didn't see them crash, but they were very close to the ground and still going down.' (Both 109s were later confirmed as destroyed.)

Several other pilots had to fight their way out as best they could including Neville Duke who had a particularly tough time before he managed to extricate himself. Not everyone got away as the 109s were able to exact revenge for their own losses by shooting down Sergeant S.H. Vinter in W3381. An extremely busy day was rounded off in the evening with a number of ASR sorties during which W3320 was flown by Flight Lieutenant 'Tommy' Lund.

Over the next few days bad weather prevented any major operations being carried out and 92 Squadron's Spitfires were limited to defensive patrols, with occasional forays over to France by small numbers of aircraft. W3320 was flown by Percy Beake on a convoy patrol off Beachy Head on 25 July, but was not used again until 3 August when Pilot Officer Phillips flew a Rhubarb sortie with Flight Lieutenant Lund in R6919.

The brief lull in activity had left both sides spoiling for a fight and a return to better weather on 7 August allowed Circus 67 to go ahead. The attack was to be carried out by six Blenheims of 107 Squadron on the airfield at St Omer, with 92 forming part of the escort cover Wing. The Circus operation had come about as a result of the *Luftwaffe's* reluctance to engage pure fighter sweeps. Often they preferred to stay on the ground, or keep a watching brief from a distance. By including a small number of bombers there was much more likelihood of exciting a reaction from the Germans, especially if the bombers' target happened to be their own airfield.

Garrick Squadron took off from Biggin Hill at 1030 hrs with Don Kingaby, in W3320, leading Blue Section. They flew to Manston where they joined up with the Blenheims and their close escorts and then set course for the French coast at a height of 16,000 ft. Shortly after passing Gravelines two Me 109s were seen below and Kingaby led his section into the attack while the rest of the squadron provided cover. Using his height advantage to close on the pair, he chose the right-hand 109 and fired a three-second burst from a range of 500 yards which produced several hits along its fuselage. On climbing to rejoin the squadron he was able to look briefly in the direction of his victim which was seen to be pouring black smoke and descending in a manner which suggested that its pilot had little control.

After the Blenheims had deposited their loads on St Omer, a further pair of 109s appeared on Kingaby's starboard side and launched a quarter attack. He turned towards them, their tracer passing uncomfortably close, but they were not prepared to mix it and both dived away inland. Shortly afterwards two more Me 109s passed in front at a range of 600 yards and Kingaby opened fire with cannon and machine-guns achieving a number of strikes on the leading machine. Rather than dive out of trouble, the German was stung into retaliation and turned to carry out a head-on attack. Kingaby could see the muzzle flashes as the 109 fired at him, and with a closing speed of approximately 600 mph, each pilot's nerve was tested to the full. Thankfully, none of the German's fire struck home, but the two aircraft avoided collision by only a few feet as the 109 broke away at the very last moment. Although Kingaby did fire at another 109 near Gravelines on the way out, it quickly dived away, apparently undamaged. As a footnote to the report that Kingaby subsequently filed on these combats, he stated that his ammunition did not contain any tracer rounds and he expressed the opinion that had it done so, the results would have been much more positive.

Two days later, W3320 was in the thick of things once again during a hotly contested Wing fighter sweep over Boulogne. Number 92 Squadron took off at 1720 hrs and began their climb to 25,000 ft with 'Beauty' (609), and 'Knockout' (72) Squadrons stepped up above and behind. It was not long before the *Luftwaffe* put in an appearance and at first both sides watched each other warily, waiting for the right moment to attack. Blue Section, which included Don Kingaby in the No. 3 position, chased after two Me 109s that were seen diving away inland but in doing so placed themselves in a vulnerable position down sun. Almost immediately they were attacked from behind and Kingaby was forced to break sharply, losing contact with the rest of the section. He was then set upon by four 109s but managed to lose them by selecting maximum boost and climbing into the glare of the sun. With the tactical situation in his favour once more he was able to turn the tables and attack the 109s, but they saw him coming and dived away towards the safety of a layer of altostratus at around 10,000 ft. Kingaby followed them down but was not able to get within firing range before they disappeared from view.

Breaking cloud a few miles inland near Hardelot, there was no sign of the 109s he had been chasing but he decided to hang around for a while to see if anything turned up. Positioning W3320 just below the layer of cloud, Kingaby kept a sharp lookout and soon spotted two more 109s climbing out of Le Touquet. He proceeded to stalk them until he was in an attacking position by which time the pair had climbed to about 7000 ft. The 109s were oblivious of his presence and he was able to close to within 150 yards before opening fire with cannon and machine-guns, the left-hand 109 shuddering violently under the impact of the shells and half rolling into a vertical descent, streaming glycol and black smoke.

A less experienced pilot may have been tempted to follow but Kingaby immediately climbed towards the cloud, thereby restoring his height advantage over the pilot of the remaining 109 who was going round in a steep turn looking for his partner's assailant. When he felt that the time was right, he launched his attack from the port quarter firing a two-second burst. The pilot of the 109 quickly realised his predicament and in an attempt to take the initiative, slammed his throttle shut hoping that this would make his opponent overshoot. Kingaby was not about to fall for this particular ploy and by pulling up the nose of his Spitfire and applying coarse rudder, he was able to decrease his speed and tuck in behind. The Spitfire was famed for its turning performance and it was not long before it was in a firing position. A two-second burst at less than 100 yards slammed into the Messerschmitt which rolled over lazily and dived into the ground about five miles south of Le Touquet. Having used up all of his 20mm ammunition Kingaby sought the sanctuary of the cloud once more and flew back to Biggin, landing at 1850 hrs.

The pace did not slacken for the rest of August and on the 12th, W3320 was one of thirty-two Spitfires put up by the Biggin Hill Wing to provide escort cover to six Hampdens of 106 Squadron attacking a power station at Gosnay. This was intended as a diversion to assist a large force of Blenheims who were undertaking an extremely hazardous operation which involved a deep penetration of German airspace to attack targets near Cologne. Later in the day 92 took part in a Wing fighter sweep during which Don Kingaby and Sergeant Wawn managed to shoot a few bits off an Me 109. This trip marked Kingaby's 200th operational sortie and his 50th offensive sweep.

Having had a day's rest, Kingaby and W3320 flew two more sorties on the 14th, the first of which provided target support to Blenheims attacking E-Boats off Boulogne. Although 92 Squadron was not engaged on this operation, a fighter sweep carried out later in the day produced a number of encounters. During the course of a brief but hectic exchange, Kingaby opened up on a 109 head on, but was not able to see the result of his fire as the German flashed past and quickly disappeared from view.

The Darlington Spitfire had its busiest day so far on the 16th with two fighter sweeps and a Circus to St Omer, and this was followed by three more sorties on the 19th. Shortly afterwards Don Kingaby began a well deserved period of leave and his 'faithful Spittie', as he was later to refer to it, was left in the care of his 'B' Flight colleagues. Despite the fact that it had been flown twice on the 18th by Pilot Officer Tony Bruce, for the last week in August it was used mainly by Pilot Officer Gordon Brettell.

Brettell had been a member of 92 Squadron since early April and at twenty-six years of age, was older than many of of his compatriots. He was a product of No. 2 Course at 58 Operational Training Unit (OTU) at Grangemouth, as indeed was Neville Duke, the two of them being the first wartime-trained pilots to join the squadron. For Brettell, flying Spitfires was a dream come true. He had an innate love of speed and

*Pilot Officer Gordon
Brettell.*
(Imperial War Museum
ref CH3566)

this led to him taking up motor racing during his time at University where he drove an Ulster-type Austin in the Inter-Varsity races. Later he competed at Brooklands in a lightened and modified example that had been rebuilt by the Monaco Engineering Company. Shortly after his arrival at Biggin he achieved a certain notoriety when he was placed on a court martial for flying his WAAF girlfriend over from Tangmere in his Spitfire for a squadron party. The unfortunate pair happened to disembark in front of the station commander, Group Captain 'Mongoose' Soden DFC, who took an extremely dim view of the affair. Brettell was charged with endangering one of His Majesty's fighting aeroplanes, but the charge was later dropped when another squadron pilot admitted to having done exactly the same thing. This incident may have been Group Captain Soden's inspiration for an idea he later presented to reduce the danger of pilots being 'bounced' from behind. He proposed to delete part of the armament in some aircraft, and transfer the radio equipment into the wing so that a small rear-facing seat could be installed behind the pilot. This was to be occupied by a Circus midget whose sole duty was to warn of imminent attack. Thankfully for everyone involved, not least the midgets, the scheme went the way of many other wartime 'brainwaves' which seemed like a good idea at the time, straight into the rubbish bin.

W3320 had a busy and varied week with Gordon Brettell which included a scramble on the 27th when unidentified aircraft were reported heading towards Hawkinge at 10,000ft. Its most active day occurred on the 31st when it flew three sorties, two offensive sweeps (the second flown by Sergeant Geoff Hickman), followed by an evening convoy patrol off the North Foreland.

The high level of activity throughout the month invariably led to mishaps and Walter Johnston recalls a very nasty accident that occurred on the 21st involving his good friend, Sergeant Stan Harrison:

> 'We were taxying round the perimeter track at Biggin Hill to get into position for take off and even taxying was planned after a fashion. The squadrons joined up into a Wing through a patterned take off which wasted no time and thus no petrol. Not only did we take off in squadron order, but individual aircraft taxied in a set pattern so that we all immediately went into our correct formation positions. We were second off that day with 72 leading and 609 following. Stan was immediately in front of me and we were approaching the infamous "blind" bend in the track with 72 lined up for take off and pointing towards us. They opened up and as Stan reached the bend he was hit by the outside man in 72. The prop caught his starboard wingroot, then chewed into the cockpit. I and the others just had to taxy past – as in the theatre, "the show must go on!"'

Harrison was severely injured in the collision and was taken to hospital barely alive. Johnston concludes the story which has a certain macabre humour:

> 'I went to see him that evening but was told on arrival that he had died. The Ward Sister gave me his watch together with the few contents of his pockets, saying that the watch was still going, and had been on the arm "when handed in!"'

The watch in actual fact belonged to Johnston as he had loaned it to Harrison who had left his own in his billet.

During the month of August there had been a number of personnel changes at Biggin Hill, which included the departure of Wing Commander Malan at the end of his tour of operations. His place as Wing Leader was taken by Squadron Leader Michael Robinson DFC of 609 Squadron, but he, too, was due for a rest from ops, and after a short period in charge he was replaced by 92's boss, Jamie Rankin. Command of Garrick Squadron was passed in turn to Flight Lieutenant R.M. 'Dickie' Milne DFC who had been posted in on the 8th.

September brought something of a respite from the frenetic activity of the past few weeks when a period of uncharacteristically bad weather, with mist and fog, prevented most operational flying for the first half of the month. The squadron maintained their proficiency with occasional local flying, as on the 13th when they carried out formation practice over Bromley, and later flew night circuits. In one respect at least the poor weather was welcome – on 8 September 92 Squadron celebrated a year in residence at Biggin Hill by throwing a big party with cabaret. Such was the standing of the top pilots of the day that Biggin was often frequented by stars of stage and screen including Laurence Olivier, Vivien Leigh and Jack Warner. The special guest of 92 on its anniversary bash was Noel Coward. Virtually as soon as the celebrations were over however, the squadron was given notice that within a matter of days they would be moving to Gravesend.

By the middle of September weather conditions had improved once more and this allowed Don Kingaby to renew his association with the Darlington Spitfire during a sweep on the 18th. Two similar operations were flown on the 20th and 21st, on the first of which, Sergeant Geoff Hickman was shot down in W3179 to become a PoW.

Over the next couple of days preparations were made for the squadron to leave Biggin Hill, a task that was taken on with a singular lack of enthusiasm as Don Kingaby recalled in his autobiography – *Greyhound in the Slips*:

> 'We were very brassed off about leaving Biggin Hill – it had provided the squadron with the chance to prove itself and from my own personal point of view it is definitely the luckiest station I have ever flown from. Apart from the operational side, I can also say that I enjoyed life there more than anywhere else in the RAF and I think that all who were there in those days will agree with me.'

The move was scheduled to be carried out on 24 September but despite an early start, only six aircraft made it to Gravesend before the weather closed in once again. The remaining Spitfires, including W3320, were forced to spend an extra day at Biggin and eventually joined up with the others at lunch-time on the 25th bringing to an end a period which, in the fullness of time, would be regarded as one of the finest in the squadron's long and distinguished history.

Chapter Three

Gravesend

Number 92 Squadron's new airfield was situated just to the south of the Thames estuary, but its elevated position did away with any weather problems that might otherwise have been expected from its proximity to the coast. Gravesend had opened as a civilian aerodrome in October 1932 when a school of flying was formed which offered pilot instruction up to commercial standard. It had also been the first home of Percival Aircraft Ltd, who produced the successful Gull three-seat tourer there before moving to Luton. With the cessation of civil flying at the outbreak of the Second World War, Gravesend was requisitioned by the Air Ministry to become a satellite of Biggin Hill. Officers were accommodated in the opulent surroundings of Cobham Hall, part of Lord Darnley's estate, but a lack of permanent buildings on the airfield meant that the NCO pilots had to make do with a small bungalow about a mile away. There was little of the Mess life that they had become accustomed to at Biggin, and most off duty hours were spent at 'Daniel's Den', a local pub where the cellars had been converted into a lounge so that drinking could continue even when air raids were in progress.

Although still a Sergeant, Don Kingaby was by now the senior pilot in the squadron in terms of operational experience, a factor which, in the harsh realities of war, was of paramount importance. This often placed him above higher ranking, but less experienced, Officers, as Walter Johnston reveals.

'At 92 the Sergeants were quite a mob, and were very experienced. On one trip Don Kingaby took the lead, I had lead of one flight and "Chips" Carpenter had the other, so the squadron had three NCOs in charge. We didn't fancy commissions because we knew that when our operational hours became official, we would be pushed off the next day on rest, as we were all way over the accepted 250 hours for a tour.'

By such means the squadron stayed together, but this resulted in a number of pilots continuing to fly operations long after they should have been screened.

On the last day of September weather conditions seemed suitable for

Line up of 92 Squadron pilots including Gordon Brettell (extreme left) and Don Kingaby (fifth from left). Other notables include: (L to R) Brian Kingcome (third) Jamie Rankin (ninth) Allan Wright (thirteenth) and Neville Duke (fourteenth). (Imperial War Museum ref CH3550)

a Rhubarb sortie and Don Kingaby took off from Gravesend in W3320 together with Neville Duke in AD125. Their efforts were to be frustrated as improving weather over the Channel, with a subsequent lack of cloud cover, meant that it would have been too risky to continue and the sortie had to be aborted. All-in-all, the Darlington Spitfire had had a relatively quiet life in September, but things were about to heat up again come October.

At 1130 hrs on 1 October Don Kingaby eased W3320 off the ground at the head of Blue Section for a squadron sweep of the area around Cap Gris Nez. On this occasion the intrusion was countered by a determined response from the locally based *Luftwaffe* fighters who subjected 92 to a series of sharp thrusting attacks. Without warning, Blue Section was 'bounced' by four 109s which suddenly appeared from a layer of cloud at around 13,000 ft, and Kingaby was forced to pull his aircraft up to seek the safety of the overcast above. When he sensed that the danger had passed, he descended out of the cloud and immediately saw another section of four 109s about half a mile to port and slightly below. Climbing back into the cloud again to conceal his presence, he manoeuvred towards them and timed his descent perfectly to position himself behind the gaggle, who were then intent on attacking another

32

Some of 92 Squadron's Spitfires parade for the camera. (Imperial War Museum ref CH3549)

group of Spitfires. Closing to a range of only 50 yards behind the last 109 in the group, Kingaby fired a one-second burst with both cannon and machine-guns into its belly and it fell away, glycol streaming from its punctured radiators.

Hugging the layer of cloud to protect himself from being attacked from above, Kingaby then flew some way inland, making sure not to fly straight and level for more than a second, thus maintaining a sharp lookout for enemy aircraft. It was not long until another bunch of 109s appeared away to his left, heading in his direction. Using the same successful tactics as before he was able to come up behind the group unseen and again picked the last one giving it a full four-second burst, coming around from the starboard quarter to astern at around 100 yards range. Such was the ferocity of his attack that the 109 went out of control immediately and Kingaby was forced to manoeuvre sharply to avoid debris. The 109 then plunged downwards, gyrating wildly, eventually breaking into several pieces before it hit the ground. Kingaby fired at another of the Germans, but by now they were fully aware of his proximity and he was forced to use the cloud cover once more to escape back to Gravesend. Details of these combats on 1 October were eventually cleared for publication, but the restrictions imposed by the wartime censor were such that the report did not appear in the *Northern Despatch* until 28 December 1943.

It is interesting to note that during this operation, Kingaby was quite prepared to go hunting for enemy aircraft on his own. Neville Duke, who, from time to time, flew as Kingaby's wingman, remembers that he was an extremely difficult pilot to follow and his combat reports certainly suggest that he had a habit of 'losing' his No. 2. Once the squadron was in action, Kingaby, like 'Sailor' Malan and many of the other top pilots, was particularly hard on his aircraft, and as he often flew it towards the very edge of its performance envelope, it was not easy for his wingman to stay in contact. As one of the 'Experten' of 92 Squadron, he was supremely confident in his own ability to fight and survive, and Duke also recalls that on one sweep over France, Kingaby came onto the radio to request assistance as he had, as he put it .... 'twelve-plus 109s cornered!'.

Continued good weather over the next few days allowed Fighter Command's offensive to be maintained, but 92 Squadron suffered a severe setback on the 2nd when Blue Section were badly bounced during a sweep of the area around Abbeville. Three pilots were shot down, including one of W3320's former pilots, Flight Lieutenant Lund. The loss of twenty-two-year-old 'Tommy' Lund was keenly felt as he was a long serving and very experienced member of the squadron, having been with 92 for exactly a year. A former student of Mediaeval History at Oriel College, Oxford, Lund had previously flown with 611 Squadron, and had risen within 92 Squadron to be 'B' Flight Commander. Neville Duke remembers him as being one of the nicest of people, and one who had gone to a great deal of trouble in helping both Gordon Brettell and himself to settle into squadron life when they had arrived in April.

In addition to having three pilots killed, Pilot Officer Tony Bruce's Spitfire was also badly shot up during which a cannon shell hit the top of his armour plating, sending fine metal splinters up into his neck and scalp. Despite his injuries, he managed to break free from his attacker and made it back across the Channel to crash-land near Ashford.

The *Luftwaffe* formations had comprised the familiar Messerschmitt Me 109Fs, but there were also reports of a radial-engined fighter flying with the 109s which resembled the Curtiss Hawk 75A (an obsolete American aircraft supplied to the French before the war). This of course was the Focke-Wulf Fw 190A, unofficially named *Wurger* or Butcher Bird, and Tony Bruce remembers being visited in hospital by several RAF Officers who were concerned not so much with his health, more so with information on the new German fighter. Bruce also got the distinct impression that the group had rushed down with somewhat indecent haste to extract the 'gen' while they still could.

On the following day the Biggin Hill Wing was required to form part of the escort cover Wing for Circus 105, but due to the losses of the pre-

Don Kingaby poses in the Darlington Spitfire.
(via Franks)

vious day, 92 could only put up two sections of four aircraft. Together with 72 and 609 Squadrons, they took off from their old base at Biggin Hill at 1338 hrs to link up with six Blenheims of 88 Squadron over Clacton before setting course for the target, the harbour installations at Ostend. Each section was flying in line astern, a tactical formation which, although a big improvement on the old Vic of three, still lacked the flexibilty of the open finger fours flown by the *Luftwaffe*. As usual, Don Kingaby was flying W3320, this time as Yellow 3, but on this occasion he was going to have more to contend with than normal. After having been subjected to some *flak* over the Channel, his problems really began when an electrical fault caused his R/T and reflector gunsight to fail completely. This would normally have been a valid reason to return to base, but as the squadron was already under strength, he chose to stay with them.

Because he was now out of touch with his comrades, it was even more imperative for Kingaby to keep a sharp lookout for enemy aircraft as there was a high degree of probability that the 109s would be a few thousand feet above and hidden by the glare of the sun. Walter Johnston, who was flying W3895 as Red 4, recalls subsequent events which he now acknowledges as having been the most frightening experience of his two fighter tours:

'We flew west along the Channel coast with the Blenheims on our landward (starboard) side, so we were looking over them and over the land from where enemy aircraft would have come. To our left, and above, were 609 Squadron who were covering us, the close escort, and the Blenheims. After the first run, we turned for a second run and remained on the seaward side of the Blenheims. I was on the outside section with Don, number 3, in the other and I had been conscious all the time that he had been looking at me rather a lot. I saw a gaggle up above us, to the rear and side and naturally assumed it to be 609 – after all, that was where they should have been. [This was a false assumption: 609 had already turned away from the target and the aircraft he could see were in fact Me 109s.]

'Then once again as I watched, they dropped down onto our formation at a hell of a rate of knots and I shouted out to the CO. We broke to starboard but they had anticipated our move only too well. As I hauled round, I saw Don doing the same – but almost at the same time the 109s came into his section. Sergeant Cox (Yellow 4) had his tail broken off and an explosion up front – Yellow 3 (Don) was out of the way, so they went straight into Sergeant Woods-Scawen (Yellow 2) who received a terrible amount of firepower. He just rolled over and went straight down.

'I had not seen Don since he had actually gone over the top of me. I felt I'd been hit, but couldn't find anything wrong with my aircraft to account for the "clang" and sort of "twitch" it had given. But even so I did not want to be too violent with it. I was quite suddenly in a large empty space of sky and set course gently and merrily for England. At that point I found myself being steadily overhauled by three 109s. I stuffed the nose down to get more speed, but they caught me up and went into line abreast so that whichever way I turned, I was covered. Two more joined them, and it was like a lot of cats after one mouse. I got the impression that they were indeed playing with me. The leader kept having a squirt, but was generally out of range and a lousy shot. I wondered if he was the leader that had to "make" his name safely.

'I had no place to go except downwards, and I began to think that I'd be safer if I jumped, hoping that they would not attack me in the drink. But things then changed rapidly. I saw another Spitfire to starboard and behind, coming down and lining up on the 109s. They had got careless and had become engrossed with me. It came down more or less along the line, firing like hell all the way. It went over the top in a flash, climbed, then came back again. As it flew alongside I realised it was Don Kingaby who was making signs that his R/T was u/s, and was also pointing his finger ahead and stabbing it, as if to say "Go, you so and so!", and so I did!'

As Johnston made good his getaway, Kingaby turned back into the 109s who, by now, had recovered from the shock that he had given them. He wrote in his unpublished autobiography *Greyhound in the Slips*:

'For a couple of minutes I twisted and turned and evaded their attacks, but then they started to come in on me from each quarter. If I broke away to the left or right I knew that one of them would have a sitting shot, so I rammed the stick forward and went down in a spiral dive from 22,000ft to 4,000ft. As I went down I looked over my shoulder and saw two Me109s firing at me and thought for a moment that they would collide. Then a shower of coolant mixture flew up over the instrument panel and into my face and I instantly thought that my engine had been badly hit. My only chance now was to get the hell out of it as fast as I could and hope that I would shake them off in the dive.'

A total of seven 109s were now chasing what appeared to be a fairly easy 'kill', and although safety was only 5–6 minutes away, each second seemed, to Kingaby, like an eternity, intensified by the constant nagging doubt that his engine was liable to seize at any moment. Pushing the throttle 'through the gate', he put W3320 into a shallow snaking dive in an attempt to shake off his pursuers. Thankfully his engine held out and, one by one, the 109s who were furthest away gave up their pursuit and turned for home. In contrast his nearest adversary proved to be extremely persistent and appeared determined to finish him off. After a long chase the German eventually managed to over-haul the Spitfire and Kingaby had little choice but to turn and fight. With his gunsight out of action he was at a distinct disadvantage, but he had had the forethought to have an old bead sight fitted to his air-craft which would be of use if he could get in close. Gradually the Spitfire's superior turning performance began to tell and after two

37

complete turns the situations began to be reversed. His autobiography continued:

> 'We were fighting just above the sea and when I began to throw him off my tail, he climbed above me and tried to half roll down onto me again. At the last moment he realised that he was too low down to do this, and to avoid going straight into the drink, he had to roll out again in the same direction as myself. I saw this happening and yanked the throttle back to slow down as quickly as possible. The 109 came out about 150 yards ahead of me and I let him have it from dead astern. Bits flew off him, there was a great cloud of smoke, and he went straight in. It was ironic that a few moments before he and his pals had had me "on ice" so to speak.'

Still expecting his engine to quit at any time, Kingaby was anxious to get down as soon as possible and made for the nearest airfield. There were to be no more dramas however and within a few minutes the large expanse of grass that was Manston appeared ahead, and a very relieved pilot slipped over the boundary fence to land.

After shutting down his engine Kingaby's post-flight inspection revealed the final twist as it became evident that his aircraft had survived the duelling unscathed, and had not suffered any hits at all. It transpired that the glycol that had flooded into his cockpit had not in fact come from the engine, but from a leak in the reservoir that contained de-icer fluid for the windscreen. The only damage to be found consisted of a few popped rivets on the upper surfaces of the wings caused by the extreme loads imposed during the combat. Up to now Darlington's Spitfire had been very reliable, but its recalcitrant behaviour on this particular day showed that the rigours of battle affected both man and machine. One thing was for sure, without the superlative skill of its pilot, both he and it would not have been around to fight another day.

Kingaby did not hang around long at Manston and soon flew back to base where the others were relating the day's events to Biggin's Intelligence Officer, Squadron Leader de la Torre. Walter Johnston made it back and remains convinced to this day that, but for Kingaby's timely intervention, he too would have gone the same way as Cox and Woods-Scawen. He also feels sure that Kingaby downed a couple of 109s in the mêlée, but there is no mention of this in the combat report that Kingaby subsequently submitted. In addition to having two pilots killed, two more aircraft had been written off due to the damage that they had received in the previous day's combat, which meant that in total, seven Spitfires had been lost over a two-day period. As Tony Bruce was in hospital recovering from his injuries, the squadron had thereby lost approximately a third of its strength in both pilots and aircraft.

In the last few weeks, whether they realised it or not, many pilots had pushed themselves to the absolute limit. As the most forward of Fighter Command's airfields in the south-east, Manston saw more than its fair share of emergency landings during this period, with 92 Squadron's Spitfires being regular visitors. Walter Johnston remembers giving civilian contractors working on the airfield a shock when they saw his aircraft riddled with thirty-six bullet holes, and on another occasion he landed drenched in sweat having been locked in a desperate struggle with two 109s. On leaving his Spitfire, he then had difficulty lighting a cigarette because his hands were trembling so much. As the squadron had been in continuous action since September 1940, it was clear that they were long overdue for a rest, and in early October it was announced that they would be pulled back to Digby in Lincolnshire, in Fighter Command's 12 Group.

The news, when it came, was greeted with stunned disbelief by the pilots who even though they were extremely tired, preferred to be in the front line, not kicking their heels at some operational backwater where nothing happened. In truth they were probably the least qualified to comment on the decision as very few would have been able to recognise the degree of fatigue from which they were suffering. Walter Johnston recalls an incident that took place shortly after the disastrous operation over Ostend, one that provides a succinct commentary on the pilots' mood at that time:

> 'Our nerves were just a wee bit "shot" and the CO turned to Don and I saying "Right you two, enough's enough, get off the 'drome, I don't want to see you until tomorrow afternoon." So off we went, pictures in Gravesend and finished up at "Daniel's Den" where we drank. For the only time in our lives we did something ridiculous and bought three drinks in a round – one for each of us, and the third for Cocky (Sergeant Cox), which we shared.'

There was to be one last chance to exact retribution for the losses that had been sustained and on 13 October Squadron Leader Milne shot down three Me 109s and damaged a fourth during a Circus operation. His virtuoso performance was the best by any 92 Squadron pilot in a single sortie and brought their tally since the start of the war to 193.

Seven of 92 Squadron's Spitfires in the air.
(Imperial War Museum ref CH2931)

Largely as a result of his actions during Circus 105, Don Kingaby received an unprecedented second Bar to his DFM, and he was the only Sergeant pilot to be so honoured during the whole of World War Two. As the sole remaining pilot in 92 Squadron who had fought in the Battle of Britain, it was announced that he would shortly be posted for a 'rest' period at an OTU. Although he had been dating Helen, a local girl from Bromley, for some time, and they were due to be married, with typical lack of compassion, the RAF's administrators promptly marked him down for Grangemouth in Scotland. Any feelings of injustice were then compounded when his good friend Walter Johnston, who was also due for a break from operations, was sent to Heston on the western edge of London!

Before these changeovers took effect, Kingaby was able to carry out one final Rhubarb sortie in W3320 on 16 October together with Sergeant Atkins in AD125. At one point the pair came across an Me 109 which Kingaby opened up at head on, but his fire appeared not to have any effect. Nearing the end of their endurance, they landed at Manston to refuel before returning to Gravesend, the twenty minute flight back to base bringing Kingaby's long and successful partnership with the Darlington Spitfire to an end.

Sergeant Frank Jones RCAF seated in W3320 at Gravesend, November 1941.
(via Darlington Library)

The aircraft movement card for W3320 shows that it served with 92 Squadron until 11 November, but there is nothing on squadron records to show that it was used after Kingaby's flight on 16 October. The move to Digby took place on the 20th, but W3320 was not one of the nineteen aircraft involved. It appears therefore that it was left behind at Gravesend and was used there for a short time on non-operational tasks. There is some evidence to support this as a photograph (see above) shows the aircraft with Sergeant Frank Jones RCAF sitting in the cockpit. Jones, who came from Sherbrooke, Quebec, had trained at 53 OTU Llandow and did not arrive at Gravesend until 4 November when he commenced his first tour of operations with 72 Squadron. He was destined not to fly W3320 and the photograph was probably set up merely for publicity purposes as it was released for publication by the press a year later. By this time Jones had been promoted to Flight Lieutenant and possessed a Distinguished Flying Cross (DFC) in recognition of his contribution to the defence of Malta with 249 Squadron.

Although the use that was made of W3320 in this period is not clear, it had obviously suffered some minor mishap as it was delivered to Air

Service Training at Hamble on 11 November for repair work to be carried out. This work took two weeks to complete and it was then issued to 24 MU at Tern Hill to be put into storage pending a decision on its future service.

Chapter Four

Castletown

Following its period of inactivity, W3320 was next issued to 'B' Flight of 54 Squadron on 1 March 1942. Number 54 Squadron was another long established fighter squadron having originally been formed at Castle Bromwich in May 1916. Although it had been disbanded in 1919, it was reformed in 1930 and flew Siskins, Bulldogs, Gauntlets and Gladiators before being re-equipped with Spitfires in March 1939. The squadron was well acquainted with the North East having been stationed at Catterick for various periods in 1940 and 1941, but by the time of the Darlington Spitfire's arrival, it was based at Castletown which was one of the most northerly fighter airfields in the UK.

It would be difficult to find a greater contrast to Biggin Hill with its frequent action, its local highlife and its 'stars'. All that Castletown could provide, apart from boredom and bad weather, were training flights on the few good days, and occasional, very often fruitless, chases after high flying Ju 88s. The airfield had opened in May 1940 as a satellite of Wick and was situated six miles south east of Thurso. To the north lay the important naval base of Scapa Flow and it was this that tempted the *Luftwaffe* to send over its reconnaissance aircraft to check on the dispositions of the Fleet. In addition to protecting the Navy, 54 Squadron's other main operational task was to provide air cover to merchant shipping moving between the east coast ports and the Atlantic via the Pentland Firth.

The Squadron's Spitfires had been battling against the elements since their arrival at Castletown on 19 November 1941. Strong winds which frequently disrupted flying also had the effect of spoiling the sporting instincts of some of the squadron's hotshots who were keen to improve the fare provided in the Officers' Mess. The Operations Record Book noted at the time that during such conditions even the local ducks were 'picketted down', and no one could bring himself to shoot stationary targets! Fittingly, W3320's arrival at Castletown was accompanied by the onset of gale force winds which persisted for the whole of the next week. When the gale eventually blew itself out the squadron diarist could not help but give vent to his frustrations by writing 'At long last this b...... wind has subsided and we are able to get on with some flying!' The squadron had only managed 270 hours flying for the whole of February and despite the approach of Spring, the weather would continue to be one of the major headaches of the weeks to come.

If the opportunities for entertainment were somewhat limited at Castletown, the antics of the station fire tender were guaranteed to cause amusement. It was operated by a crew who were particularly enthusiastic, but who were not averse to using it as a means of private transport in addition to its intended function. There were many occasions when it was to be seen charging around the perimeter track at breakneck speed, but no one could be quite sure whether it was chasing after a pranged aircraft, or merely off on another jaunt. The greatest enjoyment came from watching the expressions of those in flying control change from extreme concern to exasperation, as it invariably ground to a halt next to the NAAFI wagon.

Although extremely bleak due to its isolated position, Castletown did have its moments which were appreciated by one of W3320's pilots, Flight Sergeant Gordon Farquharson RCAF. As and when the weather relented, the area's natural beauty became apparent and Farquharson has fond memories of his time there. He was shortly to swap one barren landscape for another when he flew off the USS *Wasp* to join 126 Squadron in Malta, but before this he was to fly W3320 more than any other pilot in 54 Squadron. Its operational debut took place on 23 March when Farquharson flew it on a patrol around the islands of Orkney together with Sergeant Bill Gwynne (BL415), Sergeant Varney (AD453) and Pilot Officer Reveilhac (P8644).

The only real excitement that was to come the Darlington Spitfire's way during its time at Castletown occurred on 26 March but even this was far removed from the furious air battles that it had participated in over Northern France. An unidentified plot appeared on the radar screens and Gordon Farquharson, together with Sergeant Varney in AD453, scrambled at 1110 hrs to investigate. As so often happened though, the hostile aircraft was able to use its height and speed, together with judicious use of cloud cover, to frustrate the efforts of the two pilots and they were unable to get anywhere near it.

April the first was to be W3320's busiest day with 54 Squadron when it was involved in providing air cover to a number of slow moving merchant vessels as they proceeded sedately through the Pentland Firth. Starting in mid afternoon, it was airborne on three occasions with only a short break inbetween to change pilots and refuel. One of the pilots was Flight Lieutenant Eric Gibbs who was shortly to take over command, following the posting of Squadron Leader P.W. Hartley to 134 Squadron.

On 11 April, Castletown was visited by the commander of No. 14 (Fighter) Group, Air Vice-Marshal Raymond Collishaw CB, DSO, OBE, DSC, DFC who was on a tour of the Scottish fighter airfields, having been appointed Air Officer Commanding in March. Collishaw had been the third highest scoring fighter pilot in the First World War, and his dynamic and aggressive leadership was sorely needed in what was one of the least inspiring of operating environments.

The frequent periods of severe weather already referred to meant that pilots were often grounded for days, as a result of which they were not able to train to the same extent as their counterparts in the south. Being so far from the front line it was also easy for complacency to set in and these may well have been factors in a number of unnecessary accidents which 54 Squadron suffered around this time. These varied from minor prangs, to the fatal crash of a Spitfire which collided with an Army lorry on the Wick to Thurso road during simulated low level attacks.

On 19 April the Darlington Spitfire was being flown by a Free French pilot, Sergeant Le Peutrec, on a training flight that involved carrying out practice attacks on a number of gun posts. Having successfully completed his task he returned to Castletown but then made one of the most basic of flying errors by attempting to land downwind. His first approach resulted in an overshoot, but he appeared so determined to get down the second time that he failed to see two red Very lights that were fired in warning. Le Peutrec at least managed to land after his second attempt, but he touched down half way along the runway and was soon in danger of overrunning. In a desperate effort to scrub off some of his excess speed, he applied rudder, reasoning that a ground loop was preferable to going off the end of the runway. Unfortunately the Spitfire's undercarriage was not renowned for being particularly robust when abused, and it only endured this treatment for a few seconds before it collapsed.

When the dust had settled Le Peutrec got out to contemplate his aircraft, now sitting on its belly in an ignominious heap with mangled oleos and bent prop blades. If he had not seen the pyrotechnics as he was coming in to land, he was certainly aware of them afterwards, as he received a huge 'rocket' from his squadron commander and had to suffer the indignity of his logbook being endorsed with the words 'Gross Carelessness'. At first it was thought that repair work could be effected at Castletown, but on further inspection the damage was found to be more serious leading to a Cat B classification which would require removal to a specialist repair station. An aircraft salvage team was called in from 56 MU at Longtown airfield near Inverness and after dismantling, W3320 was taken away to commence what was to be a considerable period in the wilderness.

Although the Darlington Spitfire's departure from Castletown had been a premature one, 54 Squadron were themselves not to remain there much longer. Six weeks later they moved south to begin preparations for sailing to Australia where they were required to bolster the defences around Darwin against the threat of Japanese attack. In the meantime, W3320 was making slow progress towards the repair facility at Barassie on the Ayrshire coast and it finally arrived there on 5 May.

Given Darlington's pre-eminence in the development of the railways, it was perhaps appropriate that the town's Spitfire should be restored to its former glory at a works operated by one of the country's largest railway companies. The London Midland Scottish (LMS) Railway possessed a huge engineering organisation with a work force of almost 30,000, many of whom had been given over to the production of aircraft components and tanks. In addition to this work, the larger workshops at Derby and Wolverton took on the task of repairing Hampden, Whitley and Lancaster bombers, while the former Paint Shop at Barassie was converted so that it could carry out Spitfire repairs.

The Barassie scheme was formulated in late 1940, and work commenced in 1941, the first repaired Spitfire being completed on 10 October. The original work was carried out as a subcontract from Scottish Aviation Ltd at Prestwick, but from March 1942 a direct contract was given to the LMS. To facilitate delivery, a small airstrip was formed adjacent to the Works so that the aircraft could be flown out to nearby Prestwick for flight testing before being returned to the RAF. Initially it was envisaged that the Works would deal with a maximum of twelve aircraft at any one time, but this was soon exceeded, and by August 1942, W3320 was one of twenty-six Spitfires being worked on. As a result of the increased workload, it was not ready for collection until 1 November and a week later it was delivered to 12 MU at Kirkbride near Carlisle.

Kirkbride had been opened in June 1939 and was to be used throughout the war as an aircraft storage site. Its remote location adjacent to the Solway Firth meant that German bombers were unlikely to pay much attention to it, a situation that was fortuitous as large numbers of aircraft were eventually stored there. The turnover in aircraft was such that satellite landing grounds had to be opened at Wath Head and Hornby Hall, and the Air Transport Auxiliary formed No. 16 Ferry Pilots Pool at Kirkbride to deliver aircraft to RAF units as they were required and fly in others to replace them.

By an uncanny quirk of fate, Darlington's other Spitfire, AD387 *North Star*, arrived at Kirkbride the day after W3320, the only time that the two would come anywhere near to each other. Both aircraft were to have a lengthy stay until outside events decreed that they were required once again for active service. Although the two Spitfires had a lot more to contribute to the war, their paths were about to diverge considerably and they would see action in very different situations.

As was briefly mentioned in chapter 3, the Focke-Wulf Fw 190A had been seen for the first time over Northern France in early October 1941 and it had quickly become apparent that its performance put the Spitfire V at a considerable disadvantage. The extent of the advance made by the Germans with this aircraft was made clear in June 1942 when *Oberleutnant* Faber presented his Fw 190 to the RAF at Pembrey in South Wales having become hopelessly lost. He had mistaken the Bristol Channel for the English Channel and was convinced that he had landed in France right up until the point of his arrest!

During comparative trials the Spitfire V had been found to be 20–30 mph slower than the Fw 190 at all altitudes, and it had also been outclassed in terms of rate of roll and in both climb and diving performance. The only crumb of comfort for Spitfire pilots was that the Mark V proved to be superior in turning circles. As a result of its enforced exile the Darlington Spitfire had been fortunate enough to stay out of the Fw 190's way: many of its contemporaries had not been so lucky and were no longer around.

Following the Fw 190's arrival there was little that could be done in the short term to remedy the situation. The Hawker Typhoon was beset by teething troubles and was to prove to be a big disappointment as an interceptor. More powerful versions of the Spitfire using the Merlin 61 with its two-speed, two-stage supercharger were still some months away from squadron service, and the Rolls-Royce Griffon-powered Spitfire was even further down the road. In any case, it would not be feasible to replace all the Mk Vs with Mk IXs so something had to be done to wring more performance from the Spitfire V and the programme that was initiated was to decide W3320's operational future.

Rolls-Royce found that by cropping the blades of the supercharger impeller it was possible to increase maximum boost pressure to +18 lb/sq.in. at the low altitude of 5900 ft. This gain was offset however by a rapid fall off in performance above 12,000ft. Use of the so-called M-series Merlin in the Spitfire V closed the performance gap at low level with the Fw 190 and by 1942 there was certainly plenty of scope for a specialised low-altitude fighter. In addition to the urgent need for more fighter-bombers to carry out ground-attack work, daylight attacks by the medium bombers of 2 Group were increasing in intensity and in an attempt to minimise the effects of light and heavy *flak*, bombing heights were usually around 10–12,000 ft. The modified Spitfire Vs (re-designated LF for Low-Altitude Fighter) were to be used for close escort work, while the more powerful Spitfire IXs gave top cover. In addition to the low-altitude rated Merlin, many LF Vs featured clipped wings whereby the detachable tips were removed to increase the air-craft's rate of roll. This modification was by no means universal and many were to retain their classic wing profile, indeed pilot preference often dictated whether a particular aircraft had clipped wings or not. As wingtips could be replaced as easily as they could be removed, indi-vidual aircraft could be clipped or unclipped at varying stages of their service lives.

The LF V was intended to be very much a temporary measure until something better came along and many pilots were not particularly enthusiastic about having to fly it. To the terms 'clipped' and 'cropped', they added a third, 'clapped', referring to the aircraft's lack of per-formance in its former high altitude domain. The realisation that they were limited to low-altitude work while the Mark IX boys higher up were grabbing all the glory did not exactly help matters.

Back at Kirkbride W3320's long wait for a return to the action was almost over. Although approaching its second birthday, its prolonged storage meant that it was still relatively fresh, with only just over seventy operational hours on the clock. As a result it was selected as one of the Mark Vs to be converted to LF Vb standard and on 17 April 1943 it was delivered to Phillips and Powis Ltd for this work to be carried out.

The main modifications carried out were to the fuel system and the wing structure. The Spitfire had been designed as a short-range defen-sive fighter and its meagre eighty-five Imperial gallon fuel capacity was inadequate for the offensive work it was now being asked to do. Additional plumbing was therefore installed to allow an overload, or 'slipper' tank, of thirty gallon capacity to be carried. The tank was designed so that it could be jettisoned before entering combat, and a jettison lever was mounted on the starboard side of the cockpit. If the centrally-mounted tank was not required, provision was made for a bomb of up to 500 lb to be carried instead. As W3320 was now to see most of its action below 12,000 ft, its wing structure was beefed up to cater for the increased loads that it would have to contend with in the denser air at low level. Evidence of this modification could be seen in the longitudinal strakes on the upper surfaces of the wings.

The Darlington Spitfire finally emerged in its new guise in early June and was returned to Kirkbride on the 12th prior to being allocated to a new squadron. Although some pilots may not have been too keen on the Spitfire LF Vb, the RAF was desperate to have as many tactical fighters as it could get its hands on. No one knew when the Allied invasion of Europe would take place, but it could not go ahead without first achieving total air supremacy over much of Northern France. This would require a considerable period of time to wear down the opposing forces, and for the invasion to be successful, the Allies would need an overwhelming superiority in numbers of aircraft deployed. The establishment of a fighter force sufficient to cover the invasion was made more difficult by the demands of other Theatres, as these aircraft were also urgently needed for the campaigns in the Mediterranean and the Far East. As a result of such pressures, the Spitfire V would go on far longer than anyone at the time could have envisaged and would write its name even more indelibly in the annals of Royal Air Force history.

Chapter Five

Back in the fray

Preparations were made in early July 1943 for W3320 to return to active service and on the 6th it was delivered to 3501 Servicing Unit at Cranfield. Number 3501 SU provided the link between the Maintenance Units and the squadrons, and its task was to ensure that the aircraft that were passed to the front line squadrons were fit for the job. There were two distinct elements to this, as Test Pilot Flight Lieutenant James Pickering AFC explains:

> '3501 SU had – whilst I was on the unit – six test pilots. The aircraft passing through the unit were brought up to date with modifications which included metal ailerons and clipped wingtips ... and were then passed to the Test Flight where they were flown to maximum engine and airframe limits up to 20,000 ft. Aileron "float" was probably the most awkward handling factor that required adjustment. In some cases a small tweak on the trailing edge was enough, but it was easily overdone and stiffened aileron control above 300 mph.
>
> 'Most aircraft had several test flights of varying length ... brakes sometimes gave trouble, particularly if they had been used too much ... and constant speed units often required adjusting to maximum revs of 3000. If the boost pressure was low on take-off, this required immediate adjustment to make later readings. The final test included air firing at Sutton Bridge and entailed a flight of around 1 hour 30 minutes, in which all aspects could be re-tested.'

The Darlington Spitfire did not cause any particular problems for James Pickering and the other test pilots at Cranfield, and two days after its arrival, it was signed off to join 118 Squadron at Coltishall, where it became NK F of 'A' Flight.

Having been formed in 1918 as a training unit, 118 Squadron was disbanded at the end of the First World War and did not re-emerge until February 1941 when it commenced flying Spitfire Mark Is at Filton. The squadron had been stationed at Coltishall, to the northeast of Norwich, since January, and was mainly engaged on bomber escort duties, and as escort to anti-shipping strikes by Coastal Command Beaufighters. Occasionally the squadron's Spitfires provided cover to air-sea rescue Walruses which attempted to retrieve the crews of RAF and USAAF aircraft down in the sea off the Norfolk coast. Number 118 Squadron's badge left no doubt as to their association with over-water operations as it showed an old sailing ship in flames together with the motto: *Occido redeoque* (I kill and return).

Coltishall had been built in 1939/40 as part of the RAF's expansion programme and its first resident unit was 242 Squadron which was commanded at the time by Squadron Leader Douglas Bader DSO DFC. Like most other stations, its fortunes fluctuated throughout the war, and it had recently gone through a difficult period which had seen the loss of two Wing Leaders in two months. Number 118 Squadron itself had a new CO in Squadron Leader J.C. Freeborn DFC, who had flown with 74 'Tiger' Squadron in the Battle of Britain, and on 10 July Wing Commander P.B. 'Laddie' Lucas DSO DFC arrived to take over the Wing. Lucas was a seasoned fighter pilot who, a year before, had led 249 Squadron in the struggle to retain Malta. He was somewhat taken aback to discover that the squadrons were still flying with each section in the old line astern formation, and quickly used his Malta experience to impress upon Squadron and Flight Commanders the benefits of the open finger four. Under Lucas's leadership, morale quickly began to rise and he was to provide the direction and stability that transformed the Coltishall Wing into a first-class fighting unit.

During its time with 118 Squadron, W3320's regular pilot was Roy Flight who had joined the squadron as a Sergeant pilot in September 1942. He had taken part in a disastrous operation on 3 May 1943 when ten out of eleven Venturas of 487 Squadron were shot down during a raid on Amsterdam. A diversionary sweep by 11 Group squadrons was badly timed and only served to stir up a hornets' nest for the bombers and their escorts. The Spitfires and Venturas were soon fighting for their lives, but Flight's performance in destroying two Fw 190s and damaging a third was marred by the RAF's own losses which included Coltishall's Wing Leader, Wing Commander H.P. 'Cowboy' Blatchford DFC. The leader of the Venturas, Squadron Leader Leonard Trent, was subsequently awarded the Victoria Cross for his 'cool, unflinching courage and devotion to duty in the face of overwhelming odds'.

Flight's endeavours that day did not go unrecognised and shortly afterwards he left the squadron temporarily to take a short tactics course at the Fighter Leaders' School at Charmy Down. On his return to Coltishall as a newly commissioned Pilot Officer, he discovered that his usual Spitfire, EP413, had been lost on operations on 26 June and his new aircraft was to be W3320.

Four pilots of 118 Squadron: (L to R) Sergeant Roy Flight, Flight Sergeant Ken Paull RAAF, Flying Officer 'Jimmy' Talalla and Sergeant Tony Smith. (via Smith)

Although one could be forgiven for thinking that all aircraft of the same type and Mark number would have equal performance, this was not in fact the case. Roy Flight remembers the Darlington Spitfire as being one of the better examples:

'I tended to fly her whenever I could because she was a particularly nice one to fly and also because of her identifying letter F (for Flight). Though Spitfires of the same Mark were of the same specification, there was always some variation in how they flew and trimmed – some were much "sweeter" than others – and also in how fast they were (a combination of plane and engine). Presumably there were slight variations in the setting up of jigs, the care and skill of individual workers, factory standards and variations due to chance. All of these factors must have been blessed by the good fairy in the case of the Darlington Spitfire and I thoroughly enjoyed flying her.'

Flight's first operation in W3320 took place on 9 July and consisted of a 'Distil' patrol off the Dutch coast looking for enemy aircraft. In the event nothing was seen, but it was not long before the new partnership had their first taste of action together. On 18 July information was received from Army Co-operation Mustangs that a German convoy was proceeding along the Dutch coast near Den Helder. A large force of thirty-six Beaufighters from the North Coates Wing, equipped with torpedoes and rocket projectiles, was assembled, and these set out in mid afternoon with a Spitfire escort from 118, 402 and 416 Squadrons. The Mustangs had not gone unseen and the time taken to organise the strike had given the Germans plenty of time to prepare themselves. By the time the Beaus arrived they found that the convoy had taken refuge in the gap between Den Helder and Texel, and the attack had to be called off.

There was better luck in the evening when twelve rocket-equipped Beaufighters, six each from 143 and 236 Squadrons, took off for a second attempt. This time they found the convoy, led by a large merchant vessel, or *Sperrbrecher*, in open waters, at which point the German *flak* defences opened up with a formidable barrage as the Beaufighters began their climb to 2000 ft to begin their attack. The convoy had its own fighter protection which was engaged by the Spitfires of 118 and 402 Squadrons, while 416 Squadron flew top cover at 5000 ft. One of the Beaufighters that had just completed its dive was attacked by a pair of Messerschmitt Me 109Gs who were immediately set upon by Yellow Section. Flight Lieutenant John Shepherd DFC in EP549 pounced on the first one, firing three short bursts which ruptured its fuel tanks and caused it to blow up. The other enemy aircraft was then attacked by all members of the section and it, too, was quickly dispatched, hitting the sea and breaking up, the 'kill' being shared between Shepherd and Flight Sergeant 'Andy' Anderton. While all this was going on, Roy Flight in W3320 got in several good bursts at another 109 which was eventually shot down by Flight Lieutenant R.A. 'Dickie' Newbery. A fourth 109 was later destroyed by 416 Squadron, making it one of the most successful actions for some time.

The Squadron ORB describes the engagement as 'a real party' and notes that the victories were suitably celebrated in the Mess during the evening. In contrast, 118 Squadron's euphoria was not shared by the Beaufighter squadrons who had been subjected to intense and highly accurate *flak* during the attack. As the convoy had been relatively close to the shore, the Beaufighter crews had had to contend with *flak* batteries situated along the coast, as well as defensive fire from the ships. Two vessels were damaged and set on fire, but two Beaufighters were shot down, JL890 'X' of 143 Squadron and EL240 'E' of 236 Squadron. The others managed to return to base, but it was discovered that all had suffered varying degrees of *flak* damage, including one which was damaged so severely that it never flew again.

Although all low-level operations were extremely hazardous, attacks on German shipping were especially fraught with danger. Most convoys were protected by *flak* ships, which bristled with guns, and if

Number 118 Squadron minus CO at Coltishall in July 1943. Back row: (L to R) Smallbone, N. Brown, Wright, Freeman, Talalla (on nose), Paull, Spencer, Capel, Anderton. Front row: (L to R) McKinley, Flight, Liby, Dunning, F. Brown, Newbery, Shepherd, Watson, Hollingworth, Doe, Burrows (Eng Off). (via Smith)

there was no fighter opposition, it was the Spitfires' duty to suppress their fire while the Beaufighters went for the cargo vessels. This demanded great courage of the pilots as the Spitfire was not ideally suited to low-level attack, being particularly vulnerable to damage to its engine cooling system.

Flying Officer Sid Watson, who came from Ontario in Canada, had been with 118 Squadron since 10 May 1942 and was a veteran of many anti-shipping operations:

'Life with 118, as on any fighter squadron, was a unique experience and to have survived it at all is sometimes a great wonder. All those months when operating from Coltishall, across 150 miles of the treacherous North Sea, at zero feet on shipping recces, sometimes attacking armed trawlers and *flak* ships. One little 303 or a piece of shrapnel into our radiator and we had less than two minutes to decide to try and bale out or put the aircraft down on the water. Depending on the time of year, the

Flight Lieutenant Dickie Newbery with EN966 Fiducia, *the aircraft in which Flying Officer Frank Brown was shot down on 19 July 1943.* (via Smith)

chances of survival were extremely slim. Youth being what it is, I have seen pilots totally upset because they had to stay behind on certain operations, knowing full well that it could have been very dicey. The sad part of it all was the tremendous responsibility placed on the leaders, just kids themselves, who held the lives of others in their hands.'

On 19 July 118 Squadron was active again when eleven aircraft took off from Coltishall in mid-afternoon to carry out a 'Roadstead' operation along the Dutch coast commencing at Ijmuiden. As Sid Watson and his 'B' Flight colleagues flew south towards The Hook, 'A' Flight, led by 'Dickie' Newbery, turned north for Texel. Not long after, Newbery spotted two motor vessels of around 1000 tons and immediately ordered the Spitfires into the attack. During a brief but chaotic action, both steamers were badly damaged, but the ships' *flak* defences hit EN966 flown by Flying Officer Frank Brown DFC who bravely continued his attack even though his aircraft had begun to stream glycol when still 1000 yards away from the target. Afterwards he managed to coax his Spitfire up to 900 ft, but his engine soon spluttered to a halt and he was forced to bale out into the sea which was seen to have a considerable swell.

Roy Flight, who was flying as Brown's No.2 and had pressed home his own attack from 600 yards down to point blank range, watched his leader's plight with increasing concern and gallantly dropped his own dinghy which fell within fifty yards of Brown's position. He then con-

Flying Officer Sid Watson with Jenkins (rigger) and Ashdown (engine fitter).
(Watson)

tinued to put his own life at risk by circling low over the downed airman but, sadly, his actions were in vain as Brown was unable to reach the dinghy, and eventually disappeared from sight altogether. Low on fuel, Flight was forced to return knowing that his comrade had probably become entangled in the rigging lines of his parachute and had drowned.

Frank Brown's loss was a tremendous blow to the squadron and Roy Flight remembers that he was much loved by all. A fine all-round sportsman, excelling at both cricket and rugby, he had been with 118 for a considerable period and his coolness and courage in action were much admired. In its appraisal of his qualities, the Squadron diary concluded by saying that the RAF could ill afford to lose men of his calibre.

Following an uneventful shipping reconnaissance on 24 July, W3320 next took part in two Ramrod operations on the 25th the first of which involved providing rear support to an attack by Mitchells on the Fokker works in Amsterdam. The raid was successful and although a number of Me 109s put in an appearance, they made no attempt to

'Jimmy' Talalla and Roy Flight, who shared in the destruction of an Me 109G over Schiphol on 27 July 1943. (Flight)

intervene. In the evening 118's Spitfires gave withdrawal support to Bostons who raided the airfield at Schiphol, Roy Flight's only concern on this occasion being his No. 2 whose aircraft developed engine trouble on the way home.

Schiphol was again the target on the 27th and 118 Squadron was detailed to provide close escort to twelve Mitchells of 180 Squadron, together with the Spitfires of 402, 416 and 611 Squadrons. Having formed up over Coltishall, the formation set course for their objective initially 'on the deck', but at a pre-determined position over the North Sea they began to climb so that they crossed the Dutch coast at 11,000 ft. Just before the target was reached two Me 109Gs made a concerted attack on the Mitchells but were at once engaged by Flying Officer 'Jimmy' Talalla in AR450 (Blue 3), and Roy Flight in W3320 (Blue 4). Flight fired at the first 109 without success, but had better luck with the second one, attacking from the starboard beam and achieving a number of strikes along its fuselage and wing root. Talalla then came in from behind on the port quarter and fired two short bursts which also hit the 109, causing it to flick into a spin. There was no sign of any attempt by the German pilot to pull out, and it was last seen still going down out of control at around 4000 ft by Wing Commander Lucas. Squadron Leader Freeborn also had a good view of the 109 and was of the opinion that it could not possibly have recovered before hitting the ground. During the engagement Flight fired 56 rounds of 20mm, and 252 rounds of 0.303-in. ammunition. The precise make-up of

Flight's 20mm rounds is not known, but in the latter half of World War Two the 20mm rounds carried by Fighter Command's Spitfires consisted of a mix of High Explosive/Incendiary (HE/I) and Semi Armour Piercing/Incendiary (SAP/I), usually in equal proportions. SAP/I had replaced the Ball ammunition used previously as it possessed much higher lethality due to its superior penetration of armour plating.

The Darlington Spitfire was to take part in numerous missions by the medium bombers over the coming months during which time it would be associated with one type of aircraft more than any other, the Martin B-26 Marauder of the USAAF's Eighth Air Force. The twin-engined Marauder was sleek and powerful, and in their quest for speed the designers had opted for a small, highly loaded wing which caused one wag to comment that it appeared to have 'no visible means of support', a remark which invariably led to the nickname 'The Flying Prostitute'. It had entered service in Europe in May 1943 in the low-level role, but prohibitive losses had resulted in a change to medium-level attack. As yet, its crews did not have full confidence in their aircraft and also lacked operational experience.

W3320's first involvement with the Marauders came during the morning of 28 July when 118 Squadron escorted the 322nd Bomb Group to a point ten miles off the Dutch coast before returning to base. This was the 322nd's first operation since virtually being wiped out during a single attack in May and was intended as a diversion to draw enemy fighters away from the real attack going in on the coke ovens at Zeebrugge.

The next morning Roy Flight took off in W3320 from Coltishall's satellite airfield at Matlaske near Cromer as close escort to an attack by Marauders on Amsterdam. Although the top cover was engaged, the Spitfires that were tied to the bombers had a dud trip, their only concern being the behaviour of the Americans who steered an extremely erratic course towards the target. Having got to within ten miles of their objective, the Marauders then turned away, dropped their bombs in the sea, and made off to the sanctuary of their bases in Essex, leaving their escorts wondering just what was going on.

The unsatisfactory nature of this operation turned to catastrophe when 118 Squadron arrived back at Coltishall from Matlaske in the early afternoon. As they were breaking to land, two of their aircraft (AR447 and EP191) collided at low level over the airfield killing Flight Sergeant Joe Hollingworth and Pilot Officer Angus 'Bugs' Buglass. The tragic outcome of the accident came as a great shock, especially as the two pilots involved were most capable fliers and had been with 118 for many months. Both men were married, and the situation took on further poignancy as the crash was witnessed by Joe Hollingworth's wife who was expecting his child.

Such a grievous blow had to be quickly put to one side however, as another Marauder escort mission from Bradwell Bay to St Omer had been laid on for the evening. Although the Americans managed to hit their target this time, they still did not inspire much confidence in their protectors. Having arrived early at the rendezvous, they again steered a wavering course, and finally, on withdrawing, turned right instead of left which resulted in a landfall in the wrong place on the English coast. Such sloppy flying could lead to problems as was proved when a B-26 was shot down in error by Spitfires a week later after it appeared in an area where it should not have been.

The following day 118 Squadron turned their attention to Schiphol once again when they accompanied twelve Bostons of 107 Squadron on a 12 Group Ramrod. On their way to the objective, one of the Bostons suffered engine trouble and turned back, but its pilot was unable to maintain height and was forced to ditch in the North Sea. The close escort Spitfires in the meantime were beginning to wheeze a little as their height over the target was 13,250 ft. A number of Me 109s put in an appearance but were immediately engaged by the top cover Mark IXs of the Kenley Wing leaving Roy Flight in W3320 to an untroubled, though bumpy ride through the moderate to heavy *flak*.

Following a week's break from operations, W3320 endured a hectic day on 6 August during which it was airborne for a total of 4 hours 45 minutes. It had an early start when Flying Officer Peter Dunning flew a shipping reconnaissance over the North Sea near Ijmuiden, and this was followed in the evening by two ASR sorties looking for an Australian pilot from 611 Squadron who had been shot down into the sea off Den Helder. Several of the squadron's aircraft were involved in the search and eventually a red flare was spotted which gave the Spitfires the opportunity to circle overhead so that a position fix could be taken. Unfortunately it was nearly dark when the flare was seen and too late for a Walrus to attempt a rescue operation. Unable to offer any further assistance, the Spitfires were forced to return to Coltishall, and Sergeant John Jones, who had taken over search duty in W3320 from Roy Flight, touched down once again at 2300 hrs.

Sergeant Jones and W3320 were together again on 12 August for an early morning departure to Tangmere where 118 Squadron's Spitfires refuelled before another B-26 escort mission. The USAAF were making a determined effort to push the *Luftwaffe* fighters away from their coastal airfields in an attempt to take some of the pressure off the Eighth Air Force heavy bombers who were suffering increasing losses. The attack on the 12th was against Poix-Nord and over the next few days most of the *Luftwaffe* fighter bases would take a hammering. Three days later it was the turn of Woensdrecht, an operation that saw 118 use Martlesham Heath as a forward base. On its return, the squadron was informed that it was to move immediately to Westhampnett, a satellite of Tangmere that had been formed out of land acquired from the Duke of Richmond's Goodwood Estate. As the medium bombers' offensive against the airfields of Northern France was set to continue, the move meant that it would be much easier for 118 Squadron to plan their escort operations, as they would no longer be required to carry out time consuming and wasteful positioning flights.

The squadron's Spitfires were operational again the following day when they escorted Marauders in an attack on the airfield at Beaumont le Roger. Shortly after crossing the French coast near Le Treport, six Fw 190s managed to slip through the top cover and were engaged by the close escort Spitfires as they tried to attack the bombers. Together with Flying Officer Peter Dunning, Roy Flight got into a good attacking position and twice had an Fw 190 plumb in his sights at close range. For once the Darlington Spitfire was to let him down as its port cannon jammed due to a malfunction in its belt feed mechanism. This meant that each time he opened fire, the recoil from the starboard cannon slewed the aircraft in a most alarming manner and he was unable to aim accurately. Taking full advantage of his good fortune, the pilot of the 190 quickly dived away out of trouble leaving his frustrated opponent to resume his position close to the bombers. Despite the fact that the Marauders had been saved from attack, the 190s had managed to leave their mark as EP126, flown by Norwegian 2nd Lieutenant 'Jack' Liby, did not return. Nothing was heard of Liby's fate until two months later when news arrived that he had successfully evaded capture and was back in England.

After their earlier problems, the discipline of the Marauders was, by now, much improved and the protection afforded by the Spitfire escorts was much appreciated by the American crews who were now enjoying the lowest loss rates in the Eighth Air Force. Beaumont le Roger was again the target on 22 August but on this occasion the Fw 190s did manage to break through the escort screen before the Spitfires could intervene. *Pay Off*, a B-26C of the 386th Bomb Group based at Boxted, was badly hit in one engine and the bomb bay, and at once a serious fire

Flying Officer Peter Dunning enjoys a quieter moment at Coltishall in the summer of 1943.
(Smith)

broke out. As its pilot strove to hold the aircraft steady, the other members of the crew were able to bale out before the fuel tanks exploded, breaking it in two. Although the Spitfires had not been able to come to the assistance of the bombers, the Fw 190s did not escape without loss as one was shot down by an American gunner.

Having been at Westhampnett for only a week, 118 Squadron found themselves on the move again on 24 August, but on this occasion at least they did not have far to go as their new station was just down the road at Merston. Peter Dunning flew W3320 on its first operation from Merston on 30 August, escorting Venturas of 21 Squadron to attack an ammunition dump situated in a forest to the north of St Omer. No enemy aircraft were seen but Dunning noted in his logbook that the *flak* was 'b....y accurate'!

In early September the B-26 Bomb Groups, together with other Allied units, flew a series of missions against communications and airfield targets near the Channel coast under the code name 'Starkey'. This was intended to disrupt German troop movements to the Russian and Italian fronts by giving the impression that a full scale invasion was imminent, and involved a period of intensive bombing. By such means it was also hoped to assess the *Luftwaffe*'s strength in the Channel area which would assist those planning the real invasion. Number 118 Squadron was kept extremely busy and W3320 flew with the Marauders to the marshalling yards at Rouen and St Pol on the 6th and 7th, and with 2 Group Mitchells to the airfield at Vitry-en-Artois on the 8th. The climax to the deception occurred on 9 September when large numbers of landing craft set out at first light towards Boulogne. The fighter screen put up to protect the assault force included W3320, airborne at 0550 hrs for the first of two sorties, with a quick fifteen

Anonymous 64 Squadron Spitfire LF Vb, wearing identification stripes for Operation 'Starkey'. (Cooper)

minute turnround between the two to refuel. Its final contribution to 'Starkey' was an escort mission in the afternoon of the 9th to Monchy Breton airfield with the Bostons of 107 and 342 Squadrons.

Despite the number of sorties flown, the Germans were not taken in by the attempted ruse and hardly a shot was fired during the 'assault phase'. Another RAF squadron involved, No. 64, noted wryly that the laugh seemed to be with 'Jerry', although they were magnanimous enough to recognise that the operation had provided the Army with '...a pleasant little sea trip'. It is interesting to note that for the culmination of Operation 'Starkey' the Spitfires were painted with invasion markings, which consisted of two white stripes on the upper and lower surfaces of each wing, a forerunner of the identification markings used in earnest nine months later. The aircraft wore these stripes for a very brief period only and all had been removed again by 11 September.

Having been shackled to the bombers for so long, 118 Squadron revelled in the brief freedom of a fighter sweep on 13 September, which was destined to be Roy Flight's twenty-sixth and last trip in W3320. Leaving the English coast at Selsey Bill at low level, the formation then climbed to 12,000 ft over Fecamp and proceeded to look for enemy aircraft between Beaumont le Roger and Evreux. Unfortunately the *Luftwaffe* fighters were not to be tempted, the only danger coming from occasional, accurate *flak*. A radar report of enemy air activity in the Dieppe area was investigated but proved to be false.

Two days later, it was back to escort work with the Marauders as they carried out an attack on the *Luftwaffe* airfield at Merville. Since his arrival on 1 August from 616 Squadron, Flight Lieutenant Tony Drew, 118's new 'A' Flight Commander, had also been smitten by the Darlington Spitfire and had marked himself down to fly it on this operation. Roy Flight in the meantime was packing his bags for a couple of days leave, but his destination was about to be dramatically altered.

> 'I had been given two days leave and was about to depart for London. Just before take off a supernumery Flight Lieutenant, who was having trouble with his nerves and had been posted to us for "rehabilitation", pulled out. I volunteered to take his place and ended up in AR433 (NK-G). This was the least desirable plane in the squadron, normally kept in reserve. It was running a bit rough during the operation but no real problem until we got involved with some Fw 190s. When I put the throttle "through the gate" there was a large bang. I thought I had been hit, but my No. 2 assured me that I had not been hit by flak or by a fighter – the engine had just blown up! I could not see properly to fly, the windscreen and cockpit cover were covered by oil and the engine was smoking. I had no option but to bale out, coming down on the outskirts of Ypres.'

The others could only watch helplessly as his burning Spitfire fell away to crash near Bailleul, before continuing on their way back to Merston where they landed at 1845 hrs. As Roy Flight had been with the squadron for almost exactly a year and was highly esteemed by all, the mood was one of despondency, tempered only by the thought that his bale-out appeared to have been successful. From an operational point of view, the unfortunate circumstances that had resulted in his demise also meant that the squadron lost a future leader, as his per-formances in recent months had marked him down as a potential Flight Commander.

The squadron did not find out until two months later that Flight was safe as a PoW, by which time he had had plenty of time to reflect on the irony of events which had culminated in his imprisonment. While he endured the frustrations of inactivity, there was still much work for his aircraft to do, and on 18 September it was airborne on three occasions, commencing with a morning B-26 escort sortie to the airfield at Beauvais when it was flown by Flight Sergeant F.L. Spencer. In the early afternoon, Tony Drew took over for a weather reconnaissance of

Pilot Officer Bill 'Paddy' Harbison. (Harbison)

the area around Fecamp and Le Havre which was intended to assess the met. situation for another B-26 bombing mission that had been proposed for later in the day. He was accompanied by Warrant Officer Smallbone in AR453 who had the misfortune to have an undercarriage leg collapse on landing, causing him an almighty fright as his aircraft was pitched onto its belly. Over France there had been ominous signs of cumulo-nimbus build up, but Drew's report was promptly disregarded by the top brass and the B-26 mission to Beaumont le Roger was given the go ahead. At 1630 hrs W3320 took off again with Pilot Officer Bill 'Paddy' Harbison at the controls, but the weather had worsened considerably and a general re-call was made before the French coast was reached.

Within a matter of days it became apparent that Roy Flight's bad luck on the 15th was doubly ironic. Shortly afterwards his squadron was informed that they were to be pulled back from the front line, and on 19 September they commenced a move to Peterhead on the northeast coast of Scotland. Considering what happened the last time it ventured north of the border, W3320 was perhaps fortunate that 118 Squadron's Spitfire LF Vbs were required for further operations over

France. As a result, they began their long journey with a trip to West Malling where they swapped aircraft with 64 Squadron who, although they had been the first RAF Squadron to fly the Spitfire IX, had reverted to flying unmodified Mark Vbs in March 1943. Complete with their 'new' aircraft, 118 continued to fly north with mixed feelings, little knowing what was in store for them. Within a month they would have moved yet again and would be enjoying the splendours of Castletown!

Chapter Six

Coltishall

Number 64 Squadron was originally formed on 1 August 1916 at Sedgford as a training unit, but later saw action on the Western Front during which time it flew DH 5s and SE 5as. Like many other squadrons it was disbanded at the end of the First World War, and was not reformed until 1 March 1936, when it commenced flying Hawker Demons at Heliopolis in Egypt. Having returned to the UK, the squadron began to fly Spitfires in April 1940, and at the time of the Darlington Spitfire's arrival had only recently returned south having spent the summer at Ayr.

With the arrival of their new aircraft the pilots were naturally keen to try them out and a note in the Squadron Operations Record Book shows that they were all pleasantly surprised at the increased performance brought about by the 'cropped blowers'. As only four of the incoming aircraft had clipped wings, the squadron diarist also expressed a preference for finding wingtips for these four, rather than have to clip all the others! The Spitfires were quickly cleaned up and new squadron codes applied, those for W3320 being SH-A. It joined 'A' Flight which was commanded by the formidable Rhodesian, Flight Lieutenant Johnny Plagis DFC and bar, whose fighting skills had been honed in the skies over Malta. Unlike its service with 92 and 118 Squadrons, W3320 did not have a regular pilot during its time with 64 and tended to be passed around among the members of the Flight for varying periods.

Having carried out cannon tests on 20 September, 64 Squadron's first operation with their new aircraft took place the following morning when they escorted Mitchell bombers of 98 Squadron on Ramrod 235 to the synthetic petrol works at Lievin, near Lens. Flying Officer David Ferraby, another of the squadron's Malta veterans flew W3320 on this operation. The so called 'Ramrods' were natural successors to the 'Circus' operations flown previously, although the primary intention was now to inflict damage on the objective, and not merely draw the *Luftwaffe* into a battle of attrition. They had evolved into huge, integrated affairs which employed large numbers of fighter squadrons in sweeping around the close and top escort squadrons, and with such

Flight Lieutenant Johnny Plagis DFC* in BL734 SH-B. (Cooper)

superiority in numbers, it was rare for the *Luftwaffe* to bother the bombers unless the conditions were in their favour.

On the 21st, broken cloud provided an ideal opportunity and around fifteen Fw 190s managed to slip through and carry out a head-on attack on the Mitchells. Number 64 Squadron's Spitfires attempted to intercept, but the 190s employed their usual hit-and-run tactics and quickly dived away out of range. The action only lasted a few seconds but in that time one of the Mitchells, FL683, was shot down, and FV944 was badly damaged and was forced to ditch in the Channel, its crew being picked up by ASR launch.

Following another Mitchell escort sortie on the 23rd to Rouen, the Darlington Spitfire next accompanied a force of seventy-two Marauders to Evreux airfield on the 24th. It was flown on this trip by an American, Flying Officer John 'Junior' Harder, who had joined the squadron in February and was one of its rising stars. The bombing proved to be extremely accurate and many direct hits were seen on the dispersal areas. On the way back a solitary Me 109G rather foolishly tried to attack the bombers but was immediately engaged by Charlie Section, which included Harder in the No. 3 position. Both he and his wingman, Sergeant de Verteuil, fired at the Messerschmitt, but it was eventually finished off by section leader Flight Lieutenant Plagis and

Flying Officer John 'Junior' Harder.
(Cooper)

crashed in a fireball on the edge of a large wood about ten miles ESE of Rouen. The remainder of the withdrawal phase was uneventful, although Harder experienced a minor technical snag on his way back to base which caused him to carry out a precautionary landing at Friston.

After an extremely short stay at West Malling, on 25 September, W3320 flew with the rest of the squadron to the familiar surroundings of Coltishall which was to be its base for the next seven months. The first operation of its second stint at Coltishall occurred on the 27th and consisted of providing withdrawal support to Eighth Air Force B-17 Flying Fortresses returning from a raid on Emden. The bombers were picked up thirty miles off Ijmuiden and were shepherded across the North Sea to a landfall at Lowestoft.

Flying from Coltishall, W3320 was set to operate once again over the forbidding North Sea and on most days, even in the foulest of weather, 64 Squadron dispatched two aircraft at low level over to the Dutch coast to conduct a sea search for enemy sea movements. If ships were seen, they reported immediately and preparations were made for a strike force of Beaufighters to be sent over to attack them. By such means Wing Commander Neil 'Nebby' Wheeler's North Coates Wing had succeeded in inflicting serious losses on enemy shipping, as a result of which the Germans had been forced to route as much seaborne cargo as possible through Emden instead of

Flying Officer Ken Calder flew the Darlington Spitfire on two of its early trips with 64 Squadron.
(Cooper)

Rotterdam. This meant that the opportunities for action along the Dutch coast were not as good as earlier in the year, and although the squadron was involved in a few shipping 'prangs', many of its reconnaissance sorties were to conclude having encountered nothing more than a few fishing boats.

On 18 October John Harder flew W3320 on an escort sortie that was to prove to be a big disappointment, but one that gave a considerable fright to one of its other pilots. In addition to relating these events, the following extracts from the Squadron ORB also give an insight into the operational flexibility that was now required from a fighter squadron:

'Lovely day. After an early call at 0530 hrs the squadron, with 611, led by Wing Commander Lucas took off at 0700 hrs for Tangmere from where they were to do Ramrod 272 acting as close escort to 72 Marauders

The Darlington Spitfire

*Flying Officer W.
Bilsland.* (Cooper)

bombing Evreux aerodrome. The squadron arrived at 0800 hrs and took off again at 0820 hrs but there was nearly a very nasty accident as one of the Norwegians of 611 Squadron taxied into Flying Officer Bilsland's aircraft and ended up with what remained of his propeller in Bilsland's cockpit, pinning him down, but quite unhurt. The show was a washout as there was 10/10 cloud the whole way so the 36 Marauders (not 72 as ordered) did not bomb.'

Bilsland's Spitfire (AR549) was written off in the incident, the other aircraft involved (BL472) was subsequently repaired. Bilsland, none the worse for his ordeal, was at the controls of the Darlington Spitfire the following day:

'Fine but inclined to be showery. Very nasty "prang" last night when a "Beau" of 141 Squadron tried to come in with one engine u/s and spun in missing the NAAFI by 20 yards and went up in a burst of flame and exploding ammunition. At 1023 hrs after briefing at 0930 hrs, we, 611 and 416 Squadrons took off as escort to 27 Beaufighters from 16 Group. The target was minesweepers expected to be at work between Ijmuiden and

Den Helder. The operation was not quite what was intended as the Beaufighters turned right on reaching the Dutch coast, beat up some fishing vessels and then just strafed the sunken *Strasburg* off Ijmuiden together with two armed merchant trawlers nearby and came home. No enemy aircraft seen, all back by 1155 hrs.'

Five days later, on 24 October, 64 Squadron turned its attention to the *Luftwaffe*'s bases once again with John Harder taking up his usual position in W3320:

'At 1415 hrs Wing Commander Lucas briefed the squadron for Ramrod 284 being 12 Mitchells on Schiphol aerodrome. We and 611 Squadron took off at 1545 hrs and made rendezvous with the bombers and the Digby Wing (402 and 416 Squadrons) at a point about 40 miles off Katvik at 11,000 ft. About 10 miles before reaching the target 10–12 Me 109s dived down behind the squadron hotly pursued by the Hornchurch Spitfire IX Bs. *Flak* was very accurate … but the bombing was plumb on dispersals. One Mitchell (FL164) fell into the sea about 50 miles off Southwold and burst into flames. Gold and Charlie sections went down to see what had happened and give fixes and thus missed the Controller giving orders for the whole squadron to go to Manston for an early morning show. Only Silver section and 611 Squadron went there.'

On 3 November W3320 was to pay a return visit to Schiphol – this time the airfield was well and truly plastered by a force of seventy-two Marauders. From this period on, maintenance problems caused its utilisation rate to fluctuate considerably and it only flew one other sortie in the month, a reconnaissance along the Dutch coast by Flying Officer J.B. Ormerod on the 25th. As a result it missed one of the squadron's most successful anti-shipping operations: one that took place after a somewhat inauspicious start.

During a Wing take off in the morning of 23 November, one of 611 Squadron's aircraft suffered engine failure and was hit by a Spitfire of 402 Squadron, writing off both, and causing a major hazard in the middle of the airfield. Pilot Officer Smiley had to rudder hard to avoid them, and then found himself taking off across the line of the rest of the squadron. This very nearly resulted in another pile-up as he became airborne, in crabwise fashion, directly in front of Squadron Leader Cassidy's section. Somehow everyone managed to miss each other and with pulse rates slowly returning to normal, they flew on to the rendezvous only to find that there had been a bit of a 'cock up' (to quote Flight Lieutenant Tony Cooper's logbook) and the Beaufighters were

Squadron Leader E. Cassidy DFC, CO of 64 Squadron November 1943 – April 1944. (Cooper)

nowhere to be seen. Despite this, the Spitfires flew on to the Dutch coast where a large convoy was spotted off Vlieland, prompting the organisation of another effort later in the day.

This second attempt took place in the early afternoon and involved the squadron in providing close escort to a force of twenty-four Beaufighters. Included among their number were four of the Darlington Spitfire's pilots, Flying Officer John Harder, Flight Lieutenant Tony Cooper, Flying Officer Bilsland and Flight Sergeant Swadling. During the attack one large cargo vessel was sunk and three more ships were hit, but three of the Beaus fell to the concentrated fire of the *flak* ships. The convoy also had protection from two Fw 190s, one of which was shot down by Johnny Plagis. An Me 109G which was later encountered south of Egmond, was shot down by Squadron Leader Cassidy, Flying Officer Kelly and Sergeant Thorne.

December saw a marked improvement in W3320's serviceability and it was eventually flown on a total of ten sorties beginning with a 'Jim Crow' patrol on the morning of the 4th. Later the same day it was flown by Flight Sergeant J.D.M. Duncan on a sweep along the Dutch coast between Ijmuiden and Egmond, but 10/10 cloud cover at 3000 ft severely curtailed the squadron's freedom of action and nothing of any interest was seen.

Although W3320 was destined to be flown by a total of twenty pilots during its service with 64 Squadron, Flight Sergeant Duncan would fly it regularly in the months ahead and would come to regard it as his own. He was twenty-two years of age, and had been brought up in Glasgow, although his family had since moved to the estate at Balado, near Loch Leven in Kinross-shire. Having joined the RAF Volunteer Reserve at nineteen, he thus embarked on a similar course to his father who had served in the Royal Flying Corps during the First World War. His basic and advanced flying training was undertaken in Canada, after which he returned to the UK and was posted to 64 Squadron in July 1943. During his first five months with the squadron he had become a firm favourite, his natural exuberance and ready smile endearing him to everyone. Despite the fact that his Christian names were John David McAlpine, he was known to his family simply as Ian, but to his squadron colleagues as 'Jock'.

On 5 December W3320 made a return to the skies over Northern France and the pilot on this occasion, appropriately enough, was a Frenchman, Lieutenant Jean Muzard. After flying down to Manston to be refuelled 64 Squadron conducted a sweep near Berck sur Mer to the south of the *Luftwaffe* fighter base at Le Touquet, but again the resident *Jagdgeschwadern* were either not bothering to intervene, or were busy elsewhere.

This shuttling to and fro was still testing the squadron's resourcefulness as once or twice each week the Coltishall Wing was required to fly south to operate from 11 Group bases. On 13 December they flew down to Bradwell Bay on the Essex coast to join up with a force of Marauders whose destination, yet again, was Schiphol. The bombing was concentrated and accurate, but the German *flak* gunners protecting the airfield were particularly proficient and they succeeded in shooting down two of the bombers.

A week later W3320 completed one of its longest trips to date when it was flown by Jock Duncan to escort B-17s on their way back from

Flight Lieutenant Tony Cooper stands in front of his regular aircraft BM514 SH-G. (Cooper)

Bremen. The rendezvous with the Americans was 190 miles out from the coast of East Anglia and the Spitfires split up into pairs to escort the stragglers. The bombers had been heavily engaged over Germany and a number of them were in difficulties including B-17F 42–29664 *Jersey Bounce Jr* of the 303rd Bomb Group based at Molesworth. Having been hit by *flak* over the target, it had then become detached from the main formation and had been the subject of numerous fighter attacks. The presence of the Spitfires prevented the *Luftwaffe* fighters from causing further damage, but it was unable to maintain height and its pilot was forced to ditch in the North Sea off Cromer. As its Spitfire escort orbited overhead transmitting for a DF fix, the crew took to their dinghy and were later picked up by a coaster. The USAAF lost twenty-seven bombers during the course of the raid and without the support given by the Spitfires, this figure would undoubtedly have been higher.

Bad weather in the days leading up to Christmas hampered operations somewhat with a Jim Crow patrol on the 21st and a sweep up the Dutch coast as far as Zandvoort on the 22nd producing no worthwhile targets. The Darlington Spitfire's year was rounded off on 30 December when Jock Duncan flew it down to Manston for refuelling, prior to escorting twenty-four Mitchells in an attack on one of the many V-1 launching sites that had been constructed in the Pas de Calais area. Number 64 Squadron had taken part in a number of similar escort operations in recent weeks including the very first attack in the offensive, that on the site at Mimoyecques to the south west of Calais on 5 November. Although fighter opposition was rare, the Germans had moved in large numbers of anti-aircraft guns to defend the sites which made life very difficult for the bombers and their close escorts.

Just after New Year weather conditions deteriorated even further and put a stop to operational flying for a few days. During this period the only activity at Coltishall was the inter-squadron football match in which 64 Squadron beat their rivals from 611 by the handsome margin of 5–1. When the weather improved, Flight Lieutenant Ted Andrews took W3320 on a Jim Crow patrol on 13 January, and the following day Jock Duncan flew from Bradwell Bay for another Ramrod to the V-1 launching site near Fruges. On this occasion 64 and 611 Squadrons had their work cut out as they were the only close escort cover for a force of fifty-four Marauders. Although the bombing mission turned out to be relatively straightforward the squadron suffered a sad loss shortly after turning for home when Flight Lieutenant Bob Poulton, 64's 'B' Flight Commander, reported glycol vapour in his cockpit and almost immediately dived straight into the ground. As there was little enemy reaction at the time it could only be assumed that he had been over-come by the fumes and had lost control. In fact, his engine had failed, and he was so seriously injured during the crash landing that he spent his time as a PoW in hospital. He was invalided home on a prisoner exchange in late 1944.

By now the RAF's Spitfires were carrying out offensive sorties well into northern Europe and concern over the aircraft's limited range had led to the development of a larger overload tank with a capacity of forty-five gallons. Although these tanks had been around for some time, squadron records would appear to show that they were only made available to the Coltishall Wing in early January 1944. To determine how they could best be used, John Harder carried out fuel and oil consumption tests on the 8th and 9th of the month which established that operations could now be flown up to, and in some cases beyond, 2½ hours duration.

Full use of the new tanks would come later however as on 19 January, 64 Squadron was stood down and became non-operational prior to transiting to Ayr on the 21st for a two week stint of gunnery practice at No.14 Armament Practice Camp. Ayr was an extremely busy airfield around this time with a rapid turnover of squadrons arriving for short detachments to sharpen up their air-to-air and air-to-ground firing skills before the momentous events that were planned for later in the year. The pilots were happy to renew old friendships, having been stationed at Ayr just six months before, but were less than enthusiastic about the weather as they were greeted by driving rain and wind.

Practice eventually got under way although Squadron Leader Chapman did not endear himself to the resident staff when he managed to shoot the target drogue away from the tug aircraft. He was not the only one to achieve this distinction, as John Harder contrived to duplicate the feat a couple of days later. After each training sortie the Spitfire's cine-camera, which operated automatically when the guns were fired, provided useful evidence on film of how successful each attack had been. As a result the instructors were able to analyse any mistakes that had been made, and offer advice to each pilot on ways to improve his overall technique.

Although not a competition as such, there was intense rivalry between the pilots to see who would be the squadron's best shot, and as the detachment moved into its final period, Ted Andrews took the lead with a strike rate of 5%. This was regarded by many as being hard to beat, but he was eventually overhauled by Squadron Leader Cassidy DFC and John Harder who were neck and neck. Appropriately enough, the CO became the squadron's 'top gun' scoring 9.5%, beating the American into second place by a mere 0.5%. After an extremely successful two weeks, the squadron flew back to Coltishall on 3 February.

After its return, W3320 was to go through the operational doldrums again in February as it was used only once by Tony Cooper on a shipping reconnaissance off Den Helder and Texel on the 15th. The squadron was having particular problems with poor serviceability around this time and its groundcrews had to work long hours to make sure that even the minimum number of aircraft were available for operations. As an indication of the problems they were facing, in the space of one week in February no less than seven aircraft had to have replacement engines fitted.

The situation was not much better in March when W3320 took part in only five operations, one of which had to be scrubbed when Pilot Officer de Verteuil encountered sea fog shortly after take off for another recce along the Dutch coast. In April the only excitement occurred on

Pilot Officer N.J. de Verteuil. (Cooper)

the 27th when Jock Duncan, together with Flying Officer Thorpe in AR292, scrambled to intercept an unidentified aircraft. The excitement of the chase soon turned into a feeling of anticlimax when the so-called intruder turned out to be an American P-47 Thunderbolt.

Although W3320 may have had a quiet time in recent weeks, the same could not be said of some of its pilots who on the night of 11/12 April, carried out a comprehensive night flying programme which eventually totalled over forty hours flying time. One of those airborne was Flight Sergeant Ralph 'Archie' Maunders who returned to Coltishall just after midnight following a night navigation exercise. He was unaware that a number of Messerschmitt Me 410 intruders of KG 51 had followed RAF bombers back from a raid on Germany, and one of them had been attracted by the movement around Coltishall. As Maunders commenced his landing approach, his aircraft shuddered

77

Flight Lieutenant Tony Cooper and Squadron Leader John MacKenzie DFC were involved in the rescue of Flight Lieutenant John Harder (right) on 18 April 1944. (Cooper)

violently under the impact of numerous cannon strikes and his engine immediately caught fire. Wasting no time he slid back the hood and baled out of the right-hand side of the cockpit, as his aircraft fell into a spin to the left. Although quite low, there was just sufficient height for his parachute to deploy fully and seconds later he hit the ground, his Spitfire crashing in flames at Skeyton, two miles from the airfield. As the German intruders tended to target bomber airfields, Maunders could consider himself unfortunate to have been attacked, but at the same time extremely lucky to have survived. His was one of just three Spitfires that were lost to such activity during the war, and of the pilots involved, Maunders was the only one to escape with his life.

Six days later on 18 April, John Harder, who by now had been promoted to Flight Lieutenant, took off in AD565 for a routine Jim Crow patrol together with his No. 2, Flying Officer Law in BL734. Half way to the Dutch coast his engine suddenly lost power and then caught fire, leaving him just enough time to gain sufficient height to bale out into the sea. Weather conditions were poor with low cloud and patches of sea mist, as a result of which Law lost sight of his leader and a rescue operation had to be set in motion. A number of aircraft from 64 and 611 Squadrons were quickly airborne to try to find him and these were supported by a Walrus and an Anson of 278 Squadron. Considering the bad visibility in the area, Harder was very fortunate to be spotted by two of 64's Spitfires flown by Squadron Leader John MacKenzie DFC, who had recently taken over as CO, and Tony Cooper. The two were able to direct an ASR launch to his position and he was picked up, cold and wet, but otherwise in perfect shape.

On 29 April 64 Squadron said goodbye to East Anglia and moved to Deanland near Brighton, a change of scene that was to bring about a marked upturn in the Darlington Spitfire's fortunes. Although it had seen little in the way of action in recent months, it was about to commence a concentrated period of activity as a prelude to the Allied invasion of Europe.

Chapter Seven

Deanland

After the relatively civilised lifestyle enjoyed by the squadron at Coltishall, Deanland came as something of a shock to the system. It had been constructed as one of the Advanced Landing Grounds needed for the build-up to the planned invasion, and as such had minimal facilities, consisting of just two runways, each laid with Sommerfeld wire mesh tracking, steel plank taxyways and four blister hangars. There was none of the usual accommodation as many of the squadrons amassed along the south coast would be required to relocate to France at very short notice, and consequently all personnel had to get used quickly to living under canvas. Within days they would have to endure their first torrential rainstorm, but in the words of the Squadron diary, everyone 'came through smiling'. Number 64 Squadron was joined at Deanland, otherwise known as 149 Airfield, by their old rivals from Coltishall, 611 Squadron, as well as 234 Squadron who flew in with their Spitfire Vbs from Bolt Head.

May 1944 was to prove to be the Darlington Spitfire's busiest month of its long operational career and it eventually flew over forty-four hours in twenty-seven sorties. Jock Duncan set the ball rolling on the 2nd with an afternoon trip to the marshalling yards at Valenciennes as escort to an attack by seventy-two B-26 Marauders. The raid was a complete success with excellent bombing results being achieved.

Over the next three days the squadron was required to fly low-level escort cover in connection with exercises taking place as part of the final preparations for D-Day. As Deanland did not have facilities for night flying, 64 operated temporarily from Tangmere and W3320 was flown on four sorties, two by Pilot Officer de Verteuil, and one each by Flight Sergeant Scott Morrison and Flight Lieutenant Tony Cooper. Although this type of flying proved to be rather mundane, Tony Cooper can still remember this particular flight even after more than fifty years. Having carried out an early morning patrol off the North Foreland, he was informed shortly after landing that he had become a father. While he had been airborne his wife had given birth to a son, Peter John, whose names would eventually be painted on the cowling of his own aircraft.

The trips get longer.
(Cooper)

The medium bombers of the RAF's 2 Group and the USAAF Ninth Air Force were extremely active in the run up to the invasion attacking coastal gun emplacements and communications targets in northern France. For every raid that took place in the designated invasion area, two were scheduled to take place further along the coast towards the Pas de Calais so as to make the Germans expect the landings in this area. To further this deception the objective for 12 May was the gun position at Ault, to the north east of Dieppe. The degree of air superiority now being achieved by the Allied air forces was such that, having escorted the bombers to the target, 64 were then free to go in at low level to deliver a strafing attack on the guns. This was the first occasion that the escort fighters were allowed to carry out a more

A 64 Squadron Spitfire LF Vb under maintenance in one of Deanland's blister hangars. (Cooper)

offensive role, and similar tactics would be used again in the coming weeks.

For the rest of the month W3320 flew one and sometimes two sorties on most days as the squadron maintained a high level of activity. On the 11th Tony Cooper flew two operations, the first from Manston as escort to Bostons attacking targets at Douai, the second a sweep of the area around Lille and Cambrai from Hawkinge, which provided support cover to attacks by B-26 Marauders. Two days later Flying Officer Smiley was at the controls for a morning trip to Tourcoing, alongside twenty-four Mitchells which carried out an attack on the town's railway yards, whilst Pilot Officer de Verteuil took over for a late afternoon operation when twelve Bostons again visited Douai.

The airfields of Northern France were still receiving regular attention from the medium bombers and both Evreux-Fauville and Lille-Vendeville were attacked by them on 24 May with W3320 in attendance. On the 29th Jock Duncan flew the Darlington Spitfire on one of the longest escort operations of its career when it accompanied a force of eighteen Mitchells in an attack on the marshalling yards at Charleroi in Belgium. With a round trip of over 400 miles, fuel management was of critical importance, but thankfully the close escort Spitfires were not engaged which helped to save their precious fuel reserves.

One of 64 Squadron's groundcrew cleans BM327 SH-F. Note the Spitfire plugged in and ready to go and tents in the background. (Cooper)

In addition to the escort of 2 Group's bombers, a number of fighter sweeps were carried out by the squadron during the month. On the 19th, Flight Sergeant Morrison flew W3320 on an operation in the Le Havre area which left one of the Seine barges considerably the worse for wear after it was involved in a strafing attack near Caudebec en Caux. Although ground-attack was extremely dangerous, it could be exhilarating at times, and was especially so on this occasion as the attack had to be delivered from ultra low-level which involved the Spitfires flying under high-tension cables.

Two days later W3320 was flown by Flying Officer Thorpe as 64 Squadron joined forces with 234 Squadron to carry out an armed reconnaissance in the area Dunkirk – Tilburg – Tirlemont on the lookout for locomotives. Having departed Deanland at 0540 hrs, the Spitfires landed at Manston to refuel and were on patrol by 0730 hrs. Maximum surprise was achieved and the Deanland Wing had a field day, claiming twelve locos destroyed, seven by 64 Squadron. All air-

*Home sweet home –
John Harder poses
next to his tent at
Deanland.* (Cooper)

craft returned safely, although BL646, one of 234's Spitfires, had a
lucky escape as it reappeared over Manston wrapped up like a
Christmas parcel. Somewhere over France it had snagged a cable which
had then sprung back and coiled itself around the fuselage, restricting
rudder movement and trapping its pilot, Lieutenant 'Mike' Bernard.
After a very careful flight home and an extremely cautious landing,
Bernard had to endure a good deal of attention, not all of it sympa-
thetic, before a large pair of wire cutters was produced to set him free.

Ground targets were to suffer again on 27 May when 64 carried out
a sweep having already escorted a bombing attack on the coastal gun
battery at Longues. Flight Sergeant Travis flew W3320 on this sortie:
he, together with the other members of the squadron, strafed a number
of *Wehrmacht* trucks that had been spotted. Shortly afterwards a sta-

Tails up for France – two Spitfires raise the dust on take-off. (Cooper)

tionary train was discovered which tempted some of the pilots to consider an attack, but as they had been warned against such targets, they thought better of it. The Germans often used what appeared to be easy targets to lure the inexperienced, and their doubts were fully justified when concealed weapons opened up with a hail of fire.

As well as all its other duties in May, W3320 was also involved in an early morning scramble on the 25th when radar picked up an unidentified contact over the Channel. Flight Sergeant Maunders took off at 0450 hrs to intercept, but the radar operators saw the intruder head back towards France before visual contact could be made. A hectic month was rounded off on the 30th when it was flown by Flight Lieutenant Ted Andrews as part of the close escort to Mitchell bombers attacking one of the bridges over the Seine at Courcelles.

The timing of the Allied landings was on everyone's mind and the clearest indication as to its date occurred on 4 June when an order came through for all aircraft to be painted in invasion markings. Pilots and ground crews set to with enthusiasm to apply the 18 inch wide black and white stripes to their aircraft, although their efforts were hampered somewhat by torrential rain in the evening. The following day Wing Commander Powell called a meeting of all three squadrons of the Deanland Wing to outline the plan of attack and reassure pilots that they would be involved from the very beginning. After this the airfield was placed under armed guard, all personnel being confined within its bounds until further notice.

As a result of its exertions during May the Darlington Spitfire had the misfortune to miss taking part in the D-Day landings on 6 June when other 64 Squadron aircraft carried out low-level cover in support of the American assault to secure Utah and Omaha beaches in

Flight Lieutenant Tony Cooper with his groundcrew. (Cooper)

Normandy. For the next two weeks all groundcrews would be fully committed in keeping the Spitfires in the air so it had to wait until some of the pressure had eased before the maintenance that it needed could be carried out. Although it was to see little action over the immediate invasion period, a number of Deanland based Spitfires failed to return so at least its enforced rest meant that it was out of harm's way.

Like all pilots in 64 Squadron, Ted Andrews flew virtually round the clock during the D-Day landings. He remembers an awesome sight, and some of the dangers that he had to face from an unlikely direction:

'I was part of the squadron which provided cover over the beachhead at "H" Hour on D-Day. I shall never forget the sight of hundreds and hundreds of vessels of every description that seemed to fill the sea between the South Coast of England and Normandy. With all the other squadrons, we provided continuous cover over the beachheads during daylight hours, every day. We came to loathe flying at dawn and dusk as

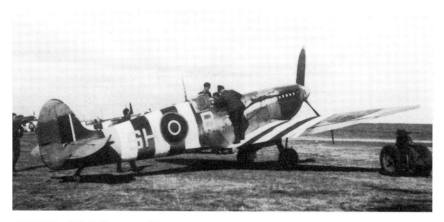

BL734 in full D-Day markings. (Cooper)

the Navy were very bad at identifying friend from foe, and they usually just pooped off and asked questions later. We lost at least two pilots in this way and the problem became so serious that a number of pilots were seconded to naval ships to educate them.'

In addition to this type of 'Friendly' fire, Flight Sergeant Ian Walker of 611 Squadron found that the USAAF were no better than the Royal Navy at aircraft recognition when he became embroiled in a dogfight over the Utah beachhead with a P-47 Thunderbolt. Luckily for him the American pilot realised his mistake before any harm was done, but this was by no means an isolated incident.

On D-Day itself Tony Cooper flew two sorties, the first at 0520 hrs. During this patrol, he too was attacked by a Thunderbolt which eventually fastened onto the tail of another Spitfire in front of him and shot it down. Cooper also witnessed a second Spitfire blowing up after being hit by a shell fired by the Navy. His overall comment was that the whole affair was like a … 'General Brocks "benefit"!'

Flight Sergeant Stan Farmiloe (who would later fly the Darlington Spitfire with 234 Squadron) recorded his D-Day experiences in a wartime diary:

'The day dawned bright and beautiful although we were up well before the first streaks of light appeared. Had quite a fitful night's sleep, some chaps reckon that they didn't sleep at all. Went out on the first show as scheduled and we were over Omaha from 0520–0610 hours, the Yanks had just started to land as we left. We saw tons of our own stuff, but no

Tony Cooper's view as he heads towards France on D-Day, 6 June 1944. (Cooper)

Jerries, it was quite a letdown – the chaps found the same thing on the second do at 0900 hours. Sims disappeared on the first trip, Lord knows what happened to him.

'Saw a wonderful sight later, we escorted a forty-five mile line of gliders and tugs to Caen, they stretched almost from the Isle of Wight to the French coast. Our biggest surprise was that there was still no enemy retaliation, everything slid along like clockwork. The gliders put up marvellous show – cast off and all landed within half a mile of one another – at least sixty gliders per field, all lined up like cars in a car park. Didn't see one crack up – damned good effort!

'I must say this has turned out to be a most surprising day. We expected to meet all the muck Jerry could put up and to have to fight for our very lives but we saw nothing – it seems almost phoney. Saw one ship hit, otherwise everything worked according to plan.'

On 7 June Tony Cooper flew three cover patrols over the Utah and Omaha beaches during which he was airborne for a total of 7 hours 25 minutes, and later recorded the following comments in his logbook:

'Beachheads established – another Airborne Division (gliders) dropped in successfully – landings continuing – Naval units bombard inland targets (Nelson, Warspite etc) – Hun tanks shelling destroyers!'

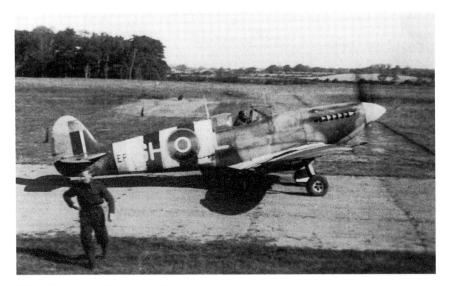

John Harder taxies out at Deanland. (Cooper)

The last operation of the three took place in the late evening and provided further evidence that it was possible to be frightened nearly as much by your own side as by the enemy:

> 'Very bad visibility – no attacks – sent forty miles out to sea on return owing to reciprocal homing vectors – very shaky experience – brought in eventually by rockets.'

By the time Cooper's section landed, it was completely dark and his No. 4 ran out of fuel as he was taxying back to dispersal. Further difficulties had been encountered over the Channel as many of the ships involved in supporting the landings had been flying anti-aircraft balloons just below the cloud base. This severely restricted the escort fighters' freedom of movement and also led to the increased risk of collision.

Of all the Deanland based Spitfires that were written off around this time, the events leading to the loss of one of 234 Squadron's aircraft were without doubt the most bizarre. During a squadron patrol to the south east of Caen, Lieutenant Bernard suffered minor *flak* damage and opted to carry out a precautionary landing near the cliff top (the fact that it was shortly after D-Day and he had not set foot in his native France for four years may also have had something to do with his decision!). As soon as the local farm workers saw his French uniform, he was feted as the returning hero and was carried off shoulder high to be toasted in the traditional French manner. Returning some time later, and slightly the worse for wear, he was horrified to discover that his Spitfire had vanished. Tracks on the ground led him to the edge of the cliff whereupon he saw his aircraft smashed to pieces on the rocks below. It transpired that an element of the British Army had come along and finding the Spitfire blocking its way, had unceremoniously dumped it over the cliff. Bernard's headache from his celebrations was thus compounded by the problem of getting home, and then having to convince his CO of a most unlikely story.

Compared to permanent RAF stations, Deanland was quite small and it became full to capacity on 8 June as the Spitfires of 350 Squadron, led by Don Kingaby, flew in to night-stop due to their own base being unserviceable. Kingaby was by now a Wing Commander and had managed to wangle his way back into the cockpit following a year at Fighter Command HQ, Bentley Priory, on a staff appointment. Whether or not he realised his old aircraft was resident at Deanland is not known, but what was evident from the part he played in the destruction of an Me 109G over Normandy on 30 June, was that he had lost none of his fighting abilities during his lengthy spell away from the action.

The honour of being the first 64 Squadron pilot to land in France went to Ted Andrews when he touched down on the emergency landing strip near Grandcamp during a patrol of the Omaha beachhead on 10 June. The other pilots were amazed to see him take off again ten minutes later, and some of the cynics among them were prompted to suggest that he had just done it to effect a line shoot for future use in the Officers' Mess. It turned out that a wing panel had become loose and had partially blocked his aircraft's radiator, causing the engine temperature to go 'off the clock'. On landing he was able to borrow a screwdriver from a passing 'Naval type', and the offending panel was removed altogether to prevent a recurrence of the problem. Despite a heart-stopping moment when an amphibious vehicle drove straight across his path as he was taking off, he was able to rejoin the squadron who were still patrolling overhead.

On the same day Flying Officer Wally 'Trapper' Smart from Winnipeg, Manitoba was heard on the radio announcing: 'I think I must have been hit, I can smell carbide'. He was quite correct – a 20mm shell had blasted a large hole measuring a foot in diameter in the fuselage of his aircraft, aft of the cockpit. Fortunately nothing vital had been hit and his Spitfire continued to fly normally. The squadron ORB

Deanland

Flak damage to Wally Smart's BM129, 10 June 1944. (Cooper)

later noted, somewhat dryly, that the hole would have been where he was sitting if he had been flying 5 mph slower! Smart was not the only pilot to have fortune on his side as Pilot Officer 'Divert' de Verteuil also collected a *flak* burst which shredded one of his tyres and caused him to nose over on landing.

In the afternoon of 16 June, 64 Squadron carried out a cover operation over the western part of the invasion area but ran into concentrated and accurate *flak* to the north west of St Lo. Several aircraft were hit including that flown by Jock Duncan which was seen to crash into a farmhouse leaving no hope that its pilot could have survived. Flight Sergeant Scott Morrison was flying in close proximity to Duncan at the time:

'We were searching for enemy road transport and/or aircraft and after reaching about fifteen miles into France we met a fair amount of flak. I was looking for enemy aircraft when I noticed Flight Sergeant Duncan's aircraft had left the squadron's attack formation and was curving away from our line of flight. I moved over to Duncan's Spitfire and saw him sitting rigidly in the cockpit while his aircraft continued to move away. I reckon Jock had been hit by an anti-aircraft shell which had killed him outright.'

91

Duncan had flown the Darlington Spitfire in the course of twenty-three operational sorties and was one of 64's most popular pilots, having been with them for nearly a year. The words written at the time in the Squadron diary convey the affection that everyone felt for him:

> 'Flight Sergeant Duncan was invaluable to the squadron in two respects. As a pilot he had won the respect and the full confidence of his colleagues, no mean part in the Air Force of today. As a man he was loved and esteemed by every member of the squadron. His happy disposition and unfailing good humour were a source of delight to all who knew him. At any time, under any conditions, "Dunc" could be relied upon to turn the bleakest prospects into a future of the rosiest hue merely by being "Dunc".'

Portentously, Duncan's great-grandmother, who many in the family believed to possess second sight, had predicted that he would 'never wear a frosty pow', an old Scottish saying meaning that he would never live to grow old. Although his death was not confirmed until after the war, it was the second tragedy to hit the family in a very short period. Just five months before, his mother, who hadn't known that her son was on active service, discovered his logbook when he returned home for a brief period of leave, and this led to her suffering a heart attack from which she subsequently died.

A week after Duncan's death, on 23 June, 64 and 611 Squadrons found themselves on the move again, this time to Harrowbeer near Plymouth. A number of Dakotas flew in to Deanland to expedite the transfer and both squadrons were operational again the following day. Harrowbeer was a little more luxurious than Deanland, having been built in 1940/41, and could at least offer three paved runways and more in the way of accommodation for personnel. After its period of inactivity, W3320 returned to the action on 24 June when it was flown by Flight Sergeant Williams as part of the cover operation to the huge amount of shipping that was now involved in re-supplying the ever-expanding bridgeheads.

Number 64 Squadron's new area of activity also covered the Brest peninsula which caused a certain amount of anxiety among its pilots as Ted Andrews recalls:

> 'We used disposable long-range fuel tanks to fly across to Brittany to provide cover for the ground forces. This was not something that we enjoyed as we were operating at the very limit of the Spitfire's range and on one occasion we only just made it back to Harrowbeer. One aircraft

'A' Flight of 64 Squadron. Back row: (L to R) *Schmitt, unknown, unknown, Recile, Thorpe. Front row:* (L to R) *Morrison, Andrews, Cooper, Smiley, Maunders.* (Cooper)

was found to have only two gallons of fuel left, which would be two minutes flying time, and all the others were down to something under ten.'

The Darlington Spitfire was to see a lot of this part of France over the next few weeks and Andrews' concerns would be shared by many of its pilots. It was not to do so with 64 Squadron however, as it flew its last operation with them on 27 June when it was flown by twenty-seven year old New Zealander, Flying Officer 'Jack' Meharry as escort to six rocket-firing Typhoons of 263 Squadron in an attack on a communications target at Pontivy. After the Typhoons had successfully carried out their strike, the Spitfires broke away to look for anything to shoot up on the way home and discovered a locomotive near the coast at Pordic. During the course of the subsequent attack, it was riddled with cannon fire and the pilots had the satisfaction of witnessing an eruption of steam from its punctured boilers which indicated the end of its useful life.

*Flight Lieutenant
H.J. Meharry.*
(Cooper)

Not surprisingly June 1944 proved to be the busiest month of the war for 64 Squadron and total hours amounted to a staggering 1150 – the bulk of which were flown in the two-week period after D-Day. Everyone had been stretched to the limit, especially the groundcrews who had to work long hours to keep the Spitfires in the air, and the pilots who had to endure the strain of continuous operations. Tony Cooper's experience was typical and involved flying up to three sorties each day. His personal total for the month was 75 hours, of which 71 were operational.

On the last day in June, Harrowbeer had an air of expectation about

Flying Officer Wally Smart stands next to John Harder's Spitfire. Note the insignia of a baby in its nappy with the name 'Junior' underneath. (Cooper)

it, which soon turned into reality with the arrival of the first batch of Spitfire IXs that were to replace 64 Squadron's trusted Mark Vs. More of the new aircraft arrived over the next few days and by 3 July, re-equipment was complete, the last Mark V sortie being flown on this date. Before the changeover there was one final tragedy with the old aircraft as the squadron lost another long serving pilot. Flying Officer Wally Smart, who had flown W3320 on two occasions and had defied death by a small margin just a few days before, was forced to return early from a shipping reconnaissance due to power loss as a result of a coolant leak. With his engine failing, he was unable to make it back to Harrowbeer and instead attempted to carry out a forced landing in a field near Loddiswell. Shortly after touchdown his Spitfire (X4257) hit

X4257, the aircraft in which Wally Smart was killed on 3 July 1944. (Cooper)

a patch of soft ground and was flipped onto its back, as a result of which Smart suffered fatal head injuries. X4257 was another long-serving Spitfire. It was first flown as a Mark I in August 1940 and was the very first to be fitted with the Type B wing with cannon armament. After conversion to LF Vb standard, it followed the same path as W3320 and flew with 118 and then 64 Squadron where it was the regular aircraft of Squadron Leader MacKenzie and was coded SH C.

The squadron's Mark Vs departed over the next few days and the majority were delivered to various second line units, including a number that were to end their days at 57 OTU which was based at Eshott in Northumberland. For the Darlington Spitfire at least there was still plenty of action to come as it was taken on charge by 611 Squadron, and on 3 July it was flown by Flight Sergeant Ian Walker to Predannack in Cornwall.

Chapter Eight

Predannack

Number 611 Squadron was formed in February 1936 as an Auxiliary unit and flew light bombers until re-designated as a fighter squadron in January 1939. Shortly afterwards it received its first Spitfires which it was to fly, in varying marks, until 1945. At the time of the Darlington Spitfire's arrival, its task was to operate over the western approaches to the English Channel and prevent enemy ships from interfering with the operation to carry supplies to the Allied forces in Normandy. The location for this work was ideal, the airfield at Predannack having been built on the heathland of the Lizard Peninsula to the south-west of Truro.

By now W3320 was coming towards the end of its useful life as a front line operational aircraft. Although still effective in its specialised low-altitude role, the increased performance and operational flexibility of the later marks of Spitfire meant that they were eagerly sought after by the squadrons that had yet to convert. By mid-1944 these aircraft were becoming much more widely available and it was only a matter of time before the old Mark Vs were pensioned off, or relegated to be used by training units.

Having been around for longer than anyone expected, the remaining Mark Vs were certainly well past their prime. By the time it joined 611 Squadron, W3320 could boast that it had flown over 160 operational sorties amounting to approximately 240 hours flying time. If test, ferry and training flights were added, this total would at the very least be doubled. It is not surprising therefore that some of 611's pilots were less than ecstatic at the thought of flying a Spitfire that was not only 'clapped' by design, but by old age as well! As things turned out they did not have to put up with the old girl for very long, as they too began to receive Spitfire IXs from 12 July.

During its short stay with 611 Squadron, W3320 was flown mainly by Flight Sergeant Ian Walker who, in contrast to some of his fellow pilots, enjoyed flying the LF Vb and remembers that it was ideally suited to the tasks that were allocated to it. After a shipping reconnaissance of the English Channel near Brest on the 4th, he flew it again three days later on a sweep of the Brest peninsula, an operation that

AR373 of 611 Squadron comes to grief. (Cooper)

was severely affected by bad weather conditions. The squadron found no enemy aircraft at Vannes airfield, and the *Luftwaffe* base at Kerlin Bastard was missed completely due to poor visibility caused by a heavy rain shower. The only potential target seen through the murk was a solitary lorry at Questembert.

On 9 July W3320 was airborne twice and was flown on both occasions by Ian Walker. Following a 40 minute sortie during which he carried out practice interceptions, Walker was one of eight pilots who took off at 1955 hrs for an armed reconnaissance of the Channel. The Spitfires were led by Squadron Leader Bill Douglas DFC and were equipped for the task with 500 lb bombs, their primary objective being to seek out enemy shipping. The squadron had flown a similar operation two weeks before but a lack of suitable targets meant that they were forced to jettison their bombs in the sea. The situation was no better this time around, but they made better use of their weaponry by attacking the radar station at Pointe du Raz as an alternative. The squadron diarist later noted, rather optimistically, that all bombs fell within the target area, but a note in Ian Walker's logbook suggests that the pilots were in need of more practice. Although he considered that the subsequent strafing attack was effective, the bombing is described as being pretty 'PP', which was an abbreviation of standard RAF descriptive slang and stood for 'Piss Poor'!

The Darlington Spitfire's fourth and last operation of its short stay with 611 Squadron occurred on 11 July when it was flown by Warrant Officer D.L. McNeil on an afternoon Rhubarb sortie. McNeil was an Australian who was generally referred to as 'Big Mac' to avoid confusion with another of the squadron's pilots, Scotsman, Flight Sergeant N.G. MacDonald, who was known in turn as 'Wee Mac'. The Spitfires were airborne at 1405 hrs and, having made a landfall at Plouescat, proceeded to attack the radio station at Callac, followed by a radar station near Botmeur. Considerable damage was caused at the latter installation with numerous strikes being observed on the *Freya* and *Würzburg* aerials, accommodation and motor transport also suffering severely.

On the following day 611 Squadron's wait for re-equipment was finally over when the first of their Spitfire IXs arrived. As a result W3320 found itself looking for a new home and it was fortunate enough to be taken on by 234 Squadron who were also based at Predannack.

Although it had been reformed in October 1939 with Blenheim fighters, 234 Squadron was to be associated with the Spitfire for much of the war, and had undergone a major transformation in October 1943 when the majority of its pilots were posted to Australia to form 549 Squadron. Since then it had taken part in numerous Ramrod and Rodeo operations over Holland and Northern France and had been kept extremely busy during the cover operations in support of the D-Day landings. Its duties at Predannack were varied and consisted of shipping reconnaissance flights and offensive sorties throughout the area of the Brest peninsula, together with occasional escort work. The squadron badge consisted of a fire-breathing dragon with the inscription *Ignem Mortemque Despuimus*, which, appropriately enough, translates as 'We Spit Fire and Death'.

By now the RAF's fighter-bombers had been given the freedom to attack anything that moved by road, rail or canal throughout the northern part of France. This had the effect of virtually paralysing the German re-supply network during daylight hours, and put their front line forces at a severe disadvantage. The highly successful attacks carried out by rocket-firing Typhoons may have taken the headlines, but the contribution of the Spitfire squadrons to the ground war was equally, if not more, important. Like any modern land army, the *Wehrmacht* had an insatiable demand for fuel, so by targetting its supply network, comprising soft-skinned vehicles, locomotives and barges, the transport of this precious commodity was restricted to an

AA936 AZ-E of 234 Squadron sports clipped wings, wing stiffening strakes and late mark exhausts. (Fairweather)

amount that represented a small fraction of the total required. Of all the German tanks and armoured vehicles that were eventually taken during the Allied advance, it was found that the majority had not been destroyed by air attack, but abandoned out of fuel. Over the next few weeks, the Darlington Spitfire would be heavily involved in this rather unglamourous, but nonetheless vital, work.

Number 234 Squadron was commanded by Squadron Leader Phil Arnott DFC, with two veterans of the air battles over Malta, Bill 'Wally' Walton and New Zealander 'Harry' Lattimer as 'A' and 'B' Flight Commanders respectively. Both were 'aces' and holders of the DFC. Also in the squadron as a supernumery Flight Lieutenant was Walter 'Johnnie' Johnston who we last met as a Sergeant pilot back in 1941 with 92 Squadron. After a spell with 61 OTU, Johnston was persuaded by 'Sailor' Malan to join him at the Central Gunnery School at Sutton Bridge as an instructor with the promise that after six months he could have an operational posting of his choice. When he arrived to join the staff, Johnston was dismayed to find that Malan had already left to become station commander at Biggin Hill and he feared that his agreement had gone with him. When his time was up he was pleased to discover that Malan had been true to his word and had left details of the arrangement with his successor at CGS. Of the available postings, Johnston chose 234 Squadron, mainly as he had known the squadron three years before at Warmwell. Sadly, Johnston was destined not to fly W3320, if he had flown the same aircraft on operations after three years, it would probably have been unique.

Although in the twilight of its career, W3320 was worked hard by 234 and eventually flew a total of forty-one operational sorties with them. It was attached to 'B' Flight and carried the code letters AZ-Y. Following the upheavals of October 1943, the squadron's make up was much more cosmopolitan which led to Darlington's Spitfire being flown by pilots from the UK and a number of Commonwealth countries. Its first outing with its new squadron occurred on 19 July when it was flown by an Australian, Pilot Officer J.R. May, on a sweep which followed the route: Plouescat – Châteaulin – Loudeac – St Brieuc. No legitimate targets presented themselves during the reconnaissance so the Spitfires dropped down to expend all of their ammunition shooting up a goods yard at Carhaix.

Although W3320 was not to have a regular pilot once again, Pilot Officer May was to fly it more than most. Despite being known as Ron back in his native Victoria, he was usually referred to on the squadron as 'Joe', even though the J in his initials stood for John. This particular nickname had come about because Squadron Leader Arnott had continually mistaken May for someone whose name actually was Joe. If this was not confusing enough, 234 already had another 'Joe' – Flight Sergeant T.P. Fargher whose real name was Philip!

Following an uneventful shipping reconnaissance, and a Jim Crow patrol that had to be abandoned due to bad weather, W3320 next set out in the evening of the 22nd to escort three Mosquitoes of 151 Squadron during a low level attack. It was flown on this operation by Flight Sergeant Stan Farmiloe whose wartime diary tells what happened:

Flight Sergeant Stan Farmiloe stands next to his regular machine, P8709 AZ-X. (Stebbings)

'This would have been a wizard do, if only I'd completed it! Three Mosquitoes carrying six 500 lb, 11-second delay bombs and eight Spits were detached to fly down to Nostang near Lorient to prang, by all methods possible, a chateau containing some Naval Headquarters. The whole show, except bombing and strafing, was to be carried out at zero feet. Half way across the Channel, Johnny Metcalfe turned back with a duff R/T and I had to return with him. First time I've ever had to come back and I was wild! The rest of them carried out the mission successfully, making quite a mess of the HQ. Mike (Bernard) was hit in the starboard mainplane by a bullet.'

On 25 July half of the squadron took part in Rhubarb 322 which involved a reconnaissance of the area around Brest. Having crossed the French coastline at Plouescat once again, the Spitfires then split up into two sections of four and proceeded to look for suitable targets. As one section contented themselves with attacking a locomotive and a number of wagons at Landivisiau, W3320, flown once again by Stan Farmiloe, was heading further to the south where twenty goods wagons were spotted to the north west of Quimper. Any means of transporting war materials or maintaining the rail system could be considered a target, although as the wagons were seen to contain some form of mineral, possibly ballast, Farmiloe was of the opinion that the attack would have had limited value. On the way back he attacked the locomotive that had already been hit by 'A' Flight leaving it, as he put it, 'rather deflated'.

On operations such as this, the long sea crossing to the French coast was often carried out at low-level to avoid radar detection and this meant flying at no more than 50 ft. One particular pilot had a reputation for flying lower than the rest and on a number of occasions he returned with damage to his Spitfire after he had inadvertantly hit the water. This could not be allowed to continue and a scheme was hatched to cure the pilot of his unfortunate habit. On return from ops one day he was engaged in conversation by some of the other pilots while a kipper was surreptitiously placed in the radiator scoop of his aircraft. He was then led around to be shown the damning evidence of yet another coming together with the sea. Suitably embarrassed, he never did it again!

The Darlington Spitfire had now been operating in the low-level role for over a year and during that time it had been fortunate to stay out of trouble. The *Luftwaffe* was now generally conspicuous by its absence, and some pilots were to complete a tour of operations without even seeing a German fighter. The main threat came from the German *flak* defences, which were potentially lethal, and the inherent danger of low-level ops was brought home to the squadron during an evening sweep on 27 July. After crossing the Channel at wave-top height, the Spitfires then climbed rapidly up to 6000 ft and proceeded to their first objective, the airfield at Kerlin Bastard. Swooping down once again, they carried out a strafing attack and then flew on further round the coast in the direction of Lorient. It was here that they were bracketed by intense *flak* which hit AR343 flown by Flying Officer E.R.'Ben' Lyon. His aircraft was severely damaged and dived away out of control, trapping its unfortunate pilot and preventing him from baling out. Shortly afterwards Flight Lieutenant 'Wally' Walton in BM200 was also hit, but he at least was able to retain control long enough to be able to bale out successfully. The rest of the squadron, in sombre mood, made it safely back to base.

During the morning of 1 August Stan Farmiloe was at readiness when a call came through concerning an unidentified aircraft. The following comes from his war diary:

'Scrambled from standby – was quite out of breath by the time I got to my kite. Vectored south by Eddy to intercept a bandit flying south and eighty miles away. Butler was my No. 2, but he just stooged away on his own – I've had it with him. I was flying "Y" and went up to the "gate", also dropping my extra fuel tank to obtain more speed (a silly thing to do really). I was clocking between 290–300 mph at 10,000 ft which is damn good for these kites. [The corresponding true airspeed would be approximately 335 mph.] I was then told that the bandit was forty miles due west, things looked good, and then it was eighty miles due north! It turned out to be friendly, a Coastal Command job. Quite a flap over nothing. There was a cloudless sky but it was just so hazy that I had to fly on instruments at 10,000 ft. Landed with just ten gallons left!'

The Darlington Spitfire was involved in a number of shipping reconnaissance sorties over the next few days including an early morning departure on 5 August. Operating from Predannack, 234 Squadron had to contend with the English Channel at its widest and their transit flights to and from the French coast amounted to approximately 250 miles over water. Most pilots would begin to think they could hear unusual noises coming from their engines as soon as the English coast disappeared from view, but engine problems were extremely rare, and many would thank the engineers at Rolls-Royce for that.

The morning patrol covered the 150 miles of coastline from the Ile d'Ouessant near Brest, to Cap Frehel to the south of Jersey. The Spitfires encountered a number of ships and were treated to a fair amount of *flak*, but as they were low on fuel, they were forced to divert to the nearest airfield, a mere 150 miles away at Bolt Head! Flying Officer Ray Stebbings piloted W3320 on this operation. He had only been with the squadron for a week, having arrived at Predannack on 28 July. Although twenty-seven years of age, this was Stebbings' first operational posting as he had spent a considerable period instructing in the USA. As there was by now a veritable glut of trained pilots, he considered himself very fortunate to have been given the chance to fly single-engined fighters at such an 'advanced' age.

The Darlington Spitfire was airborne again in the evening of the 5th for one of its more unusual escort operations. Having flown over to Bolt Head to be refuelled, the squadron took off to rendezvous with ten Halifax V aircraft, five each from 298 and 644 Squadrons, who were towing Hadrian gliders. They were taking part in Operation 'Dingson 35A' in which members of the French SAS were to operate in conjunction with their compatriots from the 4th French Parachute Battalion who had already been dropped near Lorient. Each glider contained a jeep together with three men and their equipment and the intention of the force was to create as much disruption as possible to German communications. Number 234 Squadron accompanied the Halifaxes, and later swept the area around Brest in case any of the locally based Focke-Wulfs put in an appearance. None were encountered, and the only danger came from light *flak* as the release point was reached.

Although the German reaction was minimal, this particular trip posed a number of problems for the Spitfire escort, and was by no means straightforward. Walter Johnston recalls that it was a bit of a 'hairy do', as the last fifty minutes of the return flight was carried out at night and the pilots had to resort to using the glare of the adjacent aircraft's exhaust flames to maintain their position. On this occasion at least, close escort really meant 'close'!

The next day W3320 was flown by Flight Lieutenant Tim Berry as the lead aircraft in a section of four on the lookout for enemy shipping around the Channel Islands. Berry was another recent arrival having been posted in from 611 Squadron to take over command of 'B' Flight following the posting of Flight Lieutenant Lattimer to Bentley Priory. The operation passed off without incident but the sortie is notable in that W3320 touched down on foreign soil for the first time when the four aircraft paid a brief visit to the airfield at Cherbourg before return-ing to Predannack.

After a period of bad weather which prevented any operational flying for three days, 234 Squadron's next venture into France was pre-ceded by a long transit flight along the south coast to Manston. They were accompanied by four Mosquitoes of 151 Squadron, led by Wing Commander Goodman, and in the evening, after refuelling and briefing, the Mosquitoes, together with their Spitfire escorts, set off to attack a factory near Rheims. The bombing proved to be accurate, the formation being troubled only by light *flak*, which was intense in the target area as well as between Calais and Dunkirk. As there was insufficient daylight to return to Predannack the squadron made a night-stop at Manston, returning the following day.

The pilots were faced with yet another hour long positioning flight on 14 August as they were required to fly to Tangmere to carry out an armed reconnaissance of the area around Paris. Another of 234's Australians, Pilot Officer Stan Halloran flew W3320 on this trip. Having departed Tangmere at 1240 hrs, the Spitfires crossed the French coast at 10,000 ft proceeding towards Paris where they descended to look for suitable targets.

By now every member of the squadron was extremely proficient in the air-to-ground role and when some railway trucks were seen near Beauvais, they peeled off in what was by now a well rehearsed pro-

Three of 234 Squadron's Australians, Reg Hooker, Stan Halloran and Roy Fairweather. (Halloran)

cedure. Their fire was accurate and numerous cannon strikes left the trucks a burning mass of twisted metal. On climbing to reform, some camouflaged vehicles were spotted which were given the same treatment. Content with their work, Halloran and the others flew back to Tangmere to refuel before making a leisurely return to Predannack in the late afternoon.

Further bad weather in the last two weeks of August meant that very little operational flying was carried out and of the two sorties flown by W3320, one was a complete washout. On the 20th a section of four aircraft were detailed to escort a VIP flight to the continent. Weather conditions were exceptionally bad, with patches of sea mist extending up to 1000 ft, so that it proved impossible to make contact with the other aircraft. The Spitfires groped around in the clag for two hours, eventually giving up and returning to base. Everyone in the squadron heaved a huge sigh of relief when a message came through to say that the VIP had arrived safely.

Although operations had to be curtailed due to the weather, training flights continued at every available opportunity, including squadron formation, cloud flying and practice interceptions, together with occasional cannon tests. Despite the fact that it was rarely used as a method of attack, the pilots were still required to carry out practice dive-bombing to maintain their proficiency. The usual technique was to commence the dive at 6–8000 ft, with bomb release at around 3000 ft. The Spitfire V was limited to an angle of dive of 40 degrees when carrying a bomb, but even so the speed built up impressively and required a hefty tug on the controls to pull out, subjecting the pilot to around 4 g. Dive bombing practice was carried out on 13 August during which Ray Stebbings, flying W3320, had the satisfaction of achieving a direct hit.

By now, the pilots were becoming increasingly unhappy with their isolated position at Predannack. The progress of the Allied armies had pushed the front line well to the east and even when flying at maximum range, the squadron's Spitfires were still over territory that was now under Allied control. As a result there was no chance of seeing any action unless the squadron was called forward to fly from bases further to the east, as it had been recently when it operated from Manston and Tangmere. The need for tactical fighters, even 234's elderly Spitfire Vs, was still great and there were smiles all round at Predannack when it was announced that they would shortly be moving to North Weald in Essex. The changeover took place on 28 August when Joe May flew W3320 to its new base which was ideally placed for it to continue operations over Northern France.

Chapter Nine

200 Not out

North Weald was a permanent station which was situated to the north-east of London, near Epping. Its history dated back to August 1916, and it first hit the headlines soon after when 2nd Lieutenant Wulstan Tempest took off in a BE 2c in the late evening of 2 October to shoot down Zeppelin L.31. The Zeppelin, which was commanded by the highly experienced *Kapitanleutnant* Heinrich Mathy, crashed near Potters Bar with the loss of all on board. The inter-war years saw many of the RAF's classic biplane fighters based at North Weald, and it continued to be one of Fighter Command's most important stations throughout World War Two, with many of the top squadrons being resident for varying periods. At the time of 234's arrival, it was home to another squadron of Spitfires, but within a month the airfield would become much more congested with the arrival of two Czech units.

The squadron suffered an early tragedy at North Weald as their mascot Sally, a Border Collie, and her five pups contracted a particularly virulent disease, which led to the death of four of the pups. The keeping of mascots was common practice among RAF squadrons in the Second World War and some achieved celebrity status and high rank, notably 609 Squadron's William de Goat who enjoyed rapid promotion, and ended the war as an Air Commodore. Happily the two survivors made a full recovery, and Sally was to live a long and active life having adopted Flying Officer Dave Ferguson as her post-war owner.

Before the focus of the war shifted further eastwards, there were a few final opportunities for the Darlington Spitfire to fly in the skies over Northern France as it had when it first entered service with 92 Squadron in the hot summer of 1941. Although it may not have been entirely unique in achieving this feat, there can have been very few other Spitfires still flying operationally that had also taken part in Fighter Command's first ventures into occupied Europe. Certainly all of 234 Squadron's other Spitfires were from later serial blocks and were younger by several months.

As a rule, the longer an aircraft remained in service, the more its performance was degraded due to minor damage to its airframe caused by constant use and regular maintenance. Such drag-inducing wear and

Sally, 234 Squadron's mascot, checks that the armourers have done their work correctly. (Stebbings)

tear was offset to a certain extent as the LF Vbs were, by now, coated in a semi-matt camouflage finish which had a considerably smoother surface than the matt paints used previously. Walter Johnston recalls that the aircraft were also regularly de-greased to rid them of smeared oil deposits, which tended to attract dust and dirt, and were then polished with beeswax to add a few more precious miles per hour. In addition many Spitfire Vs now featured improvements to the basic design which included the use of late-model multi-ejector exhausts in place of the old 'fish-tail' type, the deletion of the carburettor intake ice-guard, and a revised 'streamlined' rear-view mirror, all of which raised top speed (in the case of these mods alone, by 18mph). Perhaps the term 'clapped' that was often used by Mark V pilots stemmed more from jealousy than hard fact!

Despite their general age there was still much work to be done and on 30 August W3320 was flown by Flight Sergeant Alan 'Letch'

Morgan on a reconnaissance of the area Calais–Lille–Douai. Having crossed into France near Gravelines at 10,000 ft, the squadron kept a sharp lookout for anything that moved and eventually spotted three barges and around forty trucks near Douai. With such a concentration the Spitfires couldn't miss and many hits were observed during the course of the attack. The little ammunition that was left was later expended on two more barges, a dredger and a locomotive near Bethune.

The Squadron had more shooting practice on 1 September with two recces along the border between France and Belgium. Alan Morgan was in charge of W3320 once again for an early morning sortie, before handing over to Flight Sergeant John Crowhurst for the second. Both operations were successful and further hampered the movement of supplies by rail and barge to the beleaguered German ground forces. During the first trip Morgan attacked a goods train south-east of Roulers and also damaged three barges to the north of Ypres, whilst on the second Crowhurst shot up ten laden barges to the south-west of Courtrai. A busy day was rounded off in the evening when the squadron flew over to Manston to link up with a force of Mitchell bombers. A delayed departure from Manston however meant that they were late for the rendezvous and by the time they arrived there, the Mitchells had already gone. The squadron flew on to Beaumont hoping to catch up with their charges, but were unable to locate them.

As the Germans were continually being pushed back towards their homeland by the Allied advances, W3320 was now set to revisit the skies over Holland and on 5 September it was flown by Flying Officer 'Dick' Harry as 234 Squadron reconnoitred the area around Rotterdam. A locomotive was damaged and another left in flames, while a small steamer was also attacked and set on fire at Schoonhoven. The next day Ray Stebbings, by now a Flight Lieutenant, took off as one of a section of four for an early morning weather reconnaissance from The Hague to Ostend, via Antwerp. In addition to their primary duty, the Spitfires shot up a locomotive and destroyed a German staff car near Rotterdam. Stebbings also spotted a camouflaged site which was duly photographed for the Intelligence section to analyse on his return to North Weald, after a refuelling stop at Manston.

After two more armed recces around Rotterdam, there was a little bit of light relief on 11 September when 234's Spitfires were required to provide escort to Navy minesweepers and destroyers that were busy clearing mines from the Channel between Dunkirk and Ostend. Sections of two aircraft remained on station all day and the first of two

Number 234 Squadron at North Weald in September 1944. (Stebbings)

sorties by W3320 was flown by Joe May together with Tim Berry in EN858. It came as a pleasant change not to be shot at for once, but as the Navy had a reputation for firing at anything that came into view, May was not able to relax completely. With the power set to economical cruise, W3320 was able to stay with the ships for over two hours and achieved its longest operational flight to date.

Early the following day, Tim Berry led a section of four Spitfires, including Stan Farmiloe in W3320, over to Hendon where they joined up with Dakota FD797 of 24 Squadron, which was about to take a number of VIPs to Brussels. Everything went smoothly, and after an uneventful flight the Dakota and its protectors arrived at Brussels just after midday. Having been refuelled, the Spitfires were then required to continue their VIP escort duties with an afternoon flight to Amiens, a trip that marked W3320's 200th operational sortie. So far everything had gone without a hitch but it soon became clear that the Darlington Spitfire was in no mood to celebrate its milestone. As the section was taking off to return to North Weald, Farmiloe found that he was unable to achieve full power due to plug fouling and had to abort. His day went from bad to worse as it became clear that there were no groundcrews available to rectify the problem and the only way out was to clean the plugs himself, all twenty-four of them! By the time he had finished, it was too late to fly back so he was forced to night stop and return to North Weald the following day.

The Squadron was involved in escort work of a different nature two days later when it provided cover to Halifax and Wellington aircraft of 192 Squadron who were carrying out an 'Anti Big Ben' patrol. Big Ben was the code name of the German V-2 rocket, the first of which had fallen on Chiswick on 8 September. At first it was thought that the rockets were controlled by some form of radio guidance and 192 Squadron, which normally monitored the *Luftwaffe* night fighter control frequencies, was brought in to explore the possibilities of radio counter-measures. The V-2s were being launched from a site near The Hague and a listening watch was carried out at 15,000 ft off the Dutch coast. Pairs of aircraft were put up by 234 Squadron throughout the day and W3320 flew twice, partnering BL810 on both occasions. It was later discovered that the V-2s were in fact controlled by sophisticated gyroscopes, so the radio experts from 192 had been listening in vain. The only defence against the V-2 was to find and attack their launch sites, or better still, for the Allied armies to advance so as to push them back out of range.

After this brief respite from action, W3320 was back in the firing line again on 15 September when it was flown by Alan Morgan for another armed reconnaissance over Holland. Having made a landfall at Noordwijk, the squadron proceeded to Utrecht where they encountered a locomotive which they attacked and badly damaged together with a number of Army trucks. Later, a barge and a tug were attacked near the Dutch coast as the Spitfires crossed out over the North Sea on their way home.

Although W3320 had not played an active role in the D-Day landings, it did take part in the ill-fated Arnhem operation which was launched on 17 September. This involved the dropping of a massive airborne force into the area around Arnhem with the intention of securing a number of vital bridges. These were to be held while Montgomery's Army made a rapid thrust through Holland and Belgium to join up. If all had gone according to the plan, there would have been nothing to prevent an advance to the Rhine and beyond. By such means it was hoped that the war could be ended before the year was out, but events were to conspire against the Allies and the operation quickly turned into a disaster. Any thoughts of impending catastrophe were far from the mind of Joe May as he flew W3320 on the first day of the assault as escort to an air armada of gigantic proportions. Everything appeared to be progressing well, there was no sign of any *Luftwaffe* fighters, and the only concern was light *flak* experienced near Zaltbommel.

The Airborne Forces were taking two distinct routes towards

Arnhem and were encountering problems along their northernmost track as the Germans had positioned a number of *flak* barges near Schouwen Island. In the afternoon of the 18th, 234 Squadron carried out attacks on these positions which succeeded in keeping the gunners heads down while the lumbering transports and glider tugs passed over. The Darlington Spitfire was flown on this sortie by Flight Sergeant 'Joe' Fargher, a big Manxman who had extreme difficulty fitting into its small cockpit. Fargher's tour with 234 Squadron was packed with incident and after D-Day he had the misfortune to be shot down twice over Northern France within a month. Since then his flying had been relatively troublefree and by his standards, this particular operation posed no worries, although some of the other pilots may have disagreed. The Spitfires patrolled the route for just over an hour, during which time individual sections took it in turns to drop down and shoot up the gun posts whenever the gunners felt brave enough to show any signs of aggressive intent towards the transports.

Very soon the situation of the hard pressed ground troops in the Arnhem area became desperate, and there was worse to come as a deterioration in the weather meant that many of the tactical fighters were unable to intervene. W3320 flew twice with the rest of the squadron on the 19th and 20th but on reaching the French coast, low cloud and bad visibility were encountered, forcing an early return. Stan Farmiloe remembers that on the first of these trips the weather was so bad the squadron became hopelessly lost over France and had to request a radio bearing for home. This unfortunately took them directly over Calais at a height of only 1500 ft, the resulting *flak* barrage being easily the worst that he had experienced up to that time. Amazingly, everyone got through without a scratch.

The Darlington Spitfire's final sortie in connection with Operation 'Market Garden' occurred on the 23 September when Joe May carried out an escort patrol from Bourg Leopold to Eindhoven. The Arnhem fiasco was quickly over however, and what remained of the Airborne Forces began to withdraw two days later.

Rumours had been circulating for some time at North Weald that 234 Squadron was about to be re-equipped and there had been intense speculation as to what type of aircraft it would receive. So far all the promises of new aircraft had proved to be false alarms, but this time around it appeared that something would actually happen. Everything still remained a mystery as Joe May eased W3320 off the ground on 26 September for what was to prove to be its last sortie with the squadron. They were to provide the escort to a force of Mitchell bombers attack-

Mixture of Spitfire LF Vbs and Mustang IIIs at North Weald. AR364 AZ-W is in the foreground. (RAF Museum ref P7435)

ing a ferry at Breskens which was being used by the Germans to withdraw their ground forces in the face of the Allied advance. Although they were subjected to a moderate amount of *flak* in the target area, all managed to return safely to base.

The situation was somewhat clearer two days later when the Squadron diary announced exultantly: 'Re-equipment for certain this time, Mustang III, P-51 Persuit (*sic*) ships!' The Mustang III was equivalent to the USAAF P-51B and C and was an outstanding fighter which also possessed the range to fly deep into Germany. The *Luftwaffe* day fighter force had taken such a battering of late that Bomber Command could now contemplate carrying out daylight raids in addition to their night operations, and as a result 234 Squadron would be kept extremely busy until the end of the war as long-range escorts.

The first batch of Mustangs arrived on 29 September to a rapturous reception, which was only tempered by the realisation that the 'new' aircraft were actually second-hand, and had previously been flown by a Polish squadron. The rigours of operational flying had left their mark but this was quickly forgotten and 234's pilots were happy that they now had the equipment to play a full and active part in the remainder

Flight Lieutenant Ray Stebbings with his new Mustang III. Note Spitfire in the background with cylindrical overload tank. (Stebbings)

of the war. First impressions were that the Mustang accelerated and decelerated far more slowly than the Spitfire, and over the coming months serviceability, particularly engine snags, would cause many problems. With their new equipment the squadron's pilots were set to fly at much higher altitudes than with the Spitfire Vs and the transition was to prove painful at times. Due to the lower pressures at altitude, at least one pilot was to be reminded that a helping of baked beans did not constitute the ideal pre-flight meal!

By now there were very few Spitfire Vs still in front line service and most of 234 Squadron's old aircraft were transferred to various training units. The Darlington Spitfire was to be spared this indignity as it was taken on by 63 Squadron which was also based at North Weald, and was one of the last squadrons to fly the Mark V operationally.

Chapter Ten

Finger trouble

Number 63 Squadron, as they say, had had a 'funny old war' and had achieved the rare distinction of being disbanded soon after the war started when, in April 1940, it became a training unit. It was eventually reformed in 1942 and its last role, prior to moving to North Weald, had been to provide gunfire spotting for the Navy as they bombarded the German heavy gun batteries situated on the French coast before the D-Day landings. The squadron had been based at Lee-on-Solent for these duties, but moved to North Weald on 19 September as their new assignment was to provide escort to daylight attacks by Bomber Command on gun emplacements along the Dutch coast.

Number 63 Squadron took W3320 on charge on 5 October, and it flew its first operational sortie with them in the early morning of the 12th which involved escorting a force of eighty-six Lancasters of 1 Group during an attack on the gun batteries near Breskens. Although Antwerp had been taken by the Allies in early September, its port facilities could still not be used as the Germans held the banks of the Scheldt estuary, and the heavy guns situated along its length dominated the approaches. The Spitfires met up with the Lancasters over the North Sea and proceeded to patrol the target area until the last one had left. Flight Lieutenant J.D. Scholey, who was flying W3320 as 'Black 4', had an excellent view of some very accurate bombing which succeeded in destroying two out of the four gun emplacements. Despite a moderate amount of *flak*, all the attacking force and their escorts returned safely to their bases.

Shortly afterwards a period of bad weather set in which meant that operations were severely curtailed for the next two weeks. Whenever the weather relented sufficiently, the squadron flew the usual training routine of interceptions, formation practice and general aerobatics, but eventually the lack of operational flying led to a feeling of frustration and a longing to be back in the action. Towards the end of October there was a slight improvement in the met. situation which led to another escort operation being laid on for the 28th, a day that was to prove to be a fateful one for the Darlington Spitfire.

The Squadron's duty was to escort a large force of Halifax and

Lancaster bombers of 4 Group who were to attack the gun positions on the island of Walcheren. Once again Flight Lieutenant Scholey flew W3320, this time as 'Red 2', but as before, there was no sign of any enemy aircraft and the only danger came from *flak* defences in the target area which claimed two of the bombers. With their work complete, the four-engined heavies headed back to their bases in Yorkshire as the Spitfires left them to drop down to the familiar surroundings of North Weald. Scholey touched down again at 1105 hrs and taxied his aircraft back to its dispersal point before shutting down the engine for what was to be the final time. Sadly, having accumulated a double century of operations, W3320 was about to be run out by its own side.

By now North Weald was an extremely busy airfield with a large number of aircraft competing for a limited amount of space. In addition to 63's Spitfire Vs, there were the Mustangs of 234 Squadron, and the Spitfire IXs of two Czech squadrons, 310 and 313. With such a situation it was perhaps only a matter of time before somebody suffered from finger trouble and caused a potential disaster.

In the afternoon of 28 October, Bomber Command dispatched 733 heavy bombers to carry out an attack on Cologne. Extensive areas of the city were devastated, and serious damage was caused to power stations, rail and harbour installations. The bombers were provided with a heavy fighter escort which included the Spitfires of 310 Squadron. On their return to North Weald at dusk and in conditions of poor visibility, there was a certain amount of confusion as they found that a flarepath had not been lit to guide them in. What happened next was a typical piece of wartime Prunery, although the sequence of events might suggest that, by this stage of the war, Pilot Officer Prune had been grounded and put in charge of the signals square at North Weald.

Amid all the chaos, Flight Sergeant V. Nikl in MA228, not unreasonably, elected to make his approach in accordance with the landing T, unaware that this was set to a runway that was now out of wind. The poor conditions prevented him from realising the amount of drift that the crosswind was causing, and as a result his Spitfire touched down on the grass well off the side of the runway. Unfortunately W3320 and BL232, another of 63 Squadron's Mark Vs, had been dispersed close by and the Czech pilot was unable to prevent his aircraft ploughing into both of them.

Nikl escaped injury in the pile-up, but of the three aircraft involved, W3320 came off the worst. Having initially been written off with Cat E damage, MA228 was later re-assessed as Cat Ac, although its service records do not show any repair work or subsequent service. Category

Ac damage was also suffered by BL232, which was repaired on site and it later went on to serve with 41 OTU. The Darlington Spitfire sustained Cat B damage, which would have required another trip to a repair facility for it to be rectified, but with the war apparently progressing towards a successful conclusion, and the aircraft factories still churning out large numbers of late mark Spitfires, there was little operational necessity to patch up an old Mark Vb.

After its untimely demise the Darlington Spitfire disappears from the records and its ultimate fate is still shrouded in mystery. Air Ministry records are of no help and the census of former wartime aircraft, which was produced in June 1947, merely states that it is presumed to have been struck off charge. It may have survived for a while to be used as a spares source, but sooner or later it seems certain that it would have been broken up and scrapped. Even if it had not been involved in the accident, it is unlikely that it would have seen much more in the way of action. The final Bomber Command attack on the gun batteries at Walcheren occurred on 30 October, and the island was taken in early November. Number 63 Squadron did take part in a few more escort operations, but very soon the war moved out of its reach and for the rest of the year it flew a succession of training sorties. It was finally disbanded at North Weald on 31 January 1945.

To appreciate the significance of the Darlington Spitfire, it is necessary to compare its record with those of its contemporaries. The Mark V was produced in greater numbers than any other Spitfire variant and remained in production until mid-1943. Of those that out-lived W3320, nearly all flew with second line units or OTUs for considerable periods at the end of their active lives. Equally, there are a number of Mark Vs that achieved more air combat victories, but, for whatever reason, did not share W3320's longevity. At the time of its accident it was the oldest Spitfire Vb still flying operationally and, apart from its brief spell with 54 Squadron at Castletown, it flew exclusively over northern Europe, one of the most dangerous of operating environments.

Having survived for so long, there would be many who would describe the Darlington Spitfire as being a lucky aircraft. There is certainly something in this, and most World War Two fighter pilots would agree that fate played a large part in their survival. But it is also true that the top pilots had a better chance of surviving and, consequently, so too did their aircraft. Statistically, W3320 only had a 10 per cent chance of making it through its first three months with 92 Squadron. The fact that it did was largely down to the skill and expertise of Don Kingaby, a situation that would be repeated with other pilots throughout its life. The best pilots were careful to place themselves and their aircraft in the minimum amount of danger, whilst still getting the job done. They were also more aware of the hazards of operational flying than their less experienced comrades, and when a threat materialised, they usually reacted sooner. The difference between life and death could often be measured in a fraction of a second. If the Darlington Spitfire can be referred to as being lucky, then it was lucky to have had the pilots that were allocated to it.

The success of the Spitfire Fund as a means of generating revenue for the war effort meant that very few towns in Great Britain did not have a Spitfire to represent them during World War Two. Some of the bigger towns and cities were able to raise larger sums and, as a result, had more than one. The North East of England was no exception with Middlesbrough, Stockton, Hartlepool and Sunderland among the many to contribute. Of all the presentation aircraft from the North East however, none was to have a combat history comparable with that of W3320.

Middlesbrough's Spitfire (R7122 – *Erimus*) had already been damaged beyond repair before the Darlington Spitfire had even entered service. Hartlepool's (R7132 – *Industria*) did at least manage to last until March 1944 but spent much of its time at Castletown, before being transferred to 58 OTU. A Spitfire carrying the name 'Stockton, Thornaby, Billingham and Tees' (W3315) was wrecked in a forced landing at Gravesend in September 1941, and of the four Spitfires that were funded by Sunderland, all had been lost by January 1943. In contrast W3320 survived for nearly 3½ years and for considerable periods of that time it was in the front line, flying against the best that the German forces in the air, on the ground and at sea could throw at it. Its record is one of which the people of Darlington can be proud.

Chapter Eleven

The Pilots

It has often been recorded that presentation aircraft were flown by pilots who were local to the area from which they were funded. This unfortunately is a misconception that has probably come about due to the work of the Ministry of Aircraft Production's publicity section who were always keen to please their donors. If it had been true, one would have expected Walter Johnston, a Geordie, to have flown Spitfire Vb W3324 *Newcastle-upon-Tyne II* during his spell with 92 Squadron. Instead his regular aircraft was W3314 which carried the inscription *Hosiery Flight Leicester*!

During its service career the Darlington Spitfire was flown operationally by a total of fifty pilots many of whom would have had little idea as to where Darlington actually was. As well as pilots from the UK, it was flown by young men from Canada, Australia, New Zealand, France, the USA and Trinidad. The majority came from the Reserves of the Royal Air Force and the Commonwealth Air Forces, and when the shooting started, none knew how kind fate would be to them, or where the war would take them. Some would have fortune on their side, others would not. All would suffer the pain of losing close friends. This chapter highlights the careers of a number of the Darlington Spitfire's pilots and shows how they fared before and after they flew it.

Ted 'Taffy' Andrews

Ted Andrews' operational career commenced in April 1941 with 17 Squadron which was based at Castletown, with detachments at Elgin and Sumburgh. They were equipped with Hurricane IIas and their main duty was to protect merchant ships moving along the Scottish coast from the *Luftwaffe*'s long-range aircraft. In addition they were also used as makeshift night-fighters for the protection of Aberdeen, but Andrews recalls that the aircraft were wholly inadequate for the task, and no contact was ever made. His other memories of the period are of landing at night by the aid of goose-neck flares at Elgin, and of the 'dreadful' TR 9 radios which allowed limited reception with ground controllers, but no contact with other aircraft.

In January 1942 Andrews joined 229 Squadron in Egypt, and in late March he was one of ten 'A' Flight pilots who were transferred to Malta to bolster the island's aerial defences. The squadron's cannon-armed Hurricane IIcs were equipped for the task with early, and rather unreliable, long-range fuel tanks so that they could undertake the long sea crossing to Malta from Tobruk. It soon became clear that 229's aircraft were hopelessly outclassed by the Sicilian based Messerschmitt Me 109Fs, a situation that was exacerbated as the 109s invariably possessed dominance in terms of height which meant that, tactically, the Hurricanes were always in an inferior position.

On 5 April Andrews' BM964 was one of four Hurricanes that attempted to intercept a large raid by forty Ju 88s and fifteen Ju 87 *Stukas*. Still struggling for height, they were bounced by Me 109s and Andrews' aircraft was badly hit, seriously wounding him in the arm and leg. Despite the severity of his injuries, he succeeded in landing at Luqa, but his aircraft's hydraulics had been damaged during the attack which caused it to overrun the airfield, injuring him still further.

After spending six months in hospital he was able to fly once again, although he still had little movement in his right elbow. Initially he was restricted to non-operational flying, which consisted of acting as 'chauffeur' to VIPs, but eventually he was given clearance to fly single-engined fighters and joined 64 Squadron on 10 October 1943.

Shortly after the Darlington Spitfire's departure in July 1944, 64 Squadron moved to Bradwell Bay in Essex where they were involved in numerous escort and armed reconnaissance operations, together with occasional chases after V-1 flying bombs. As the cruising speed of the V-1 was nearly 400 mph, Andrews recalls that they could only be caught by a Spitfire IX in a dive, and that their small size made them very difficult to spot from above.

In November 1944 Andrews was posted to 154 Squadron which reformed at Biggin Hill on the 16th with Spitfire HF.VIIs. These were swapped for Mustang IVs soon after the squadron became operational and their primary duty was then to escort daylight attacks by Lancasters deep into Germany. It was during one of these operations to Dortmund on 12 March that Andrews experienced engine failure in KH721 and was forced to bale out to spend the last few weeks of the war as a PoW. He was to have one last brush with death when he suffered head injuries after a low flying Typhoon mistook a column of prisoners for German soldiers and opened fire.

Percy Beake

Beake was brought up in Bristol, where he attended Victoria Park School and Bristol Grammar School, before joining the Royal Air Force Volunteer Reserve in April 1939. His first taste of flying came courtesy of the ubiquitous Tiger Moth at the nearby airfield of Whitchurch, after which he underwent further basic training at Redhill, before graduating onto Harvards at 15 SFTS, Chipping Norton, and Masters/Spitfires at 7 OTU, Hawarden.

His first operational posting was to 64 Squadron at Leconfield on 22 September 1940, but two months later they moved south and commenced operations over France as part of the Hornchurch Wing. In May 1941 the squadron was pulled back to Turnhouse, near Edinburgh, where there was little in the way of action, and the pilots had to be content mainly with convoy protection duties. Such mundane work meant that morale quickly began to drop, and the frustrations were typified by a sortie that Beake flew on 21 May, one that involved carrying out practice attacks on an Army gunpost. Arriving overhead at the appointed time, he proceeded to attack the post as briefed, but noticed that the gunners were tucking into their lunches. Despite his best efforts, which had been laid on especially for the gun-crews benefit, they steadfastly refused to stop eating their sandwiches, and took no notice of him at all!

On 27 June 1941 Beake moved to 92 Squadron, where he flew W3320 on two operations, before transferring to 601 Squadron at Acaster Malbis in Yorkshire in early 1942. Here he had the rather dubious honour of helping to introduce the Bell Airacobra into RAF service, a task that was made extremely difficult due to poor serviceability and numerous crashes. Eventually it was decided that the American aircraft would never make it as first-line equipment and they were replaced by Spitfire Vbs. Shortly afterwards Beake's first tour came to an end and in March 1942 he commenced a 'rest' period instructing at 58 OTU, Grangemouth.

Having been promoted to Flight Lieutenant, he returned to ops as a Flight Commander with 193 Squadron in December, commencing what was to be a long association with the Hawker Typhoon which saw him take command of 164 Squadron at Thorney Island in May 1944. The Typhoon was an excellent performer at low level and on D-Day itself, Beake shot down an Fw 190 on a patrol to the east of Caen when flying DN432 (FJ F). This was the squadron's first confirmed 'kill' of the war. The squadron moved to the forward airfield at Sommervieu

(B. 8) in July, quickly transferring to Martragny (B. 7) from where they flew 'cab rank' sorties against enemy tanks and troop concentrations. Beake continued to lead the squadron until September when he was posted to the Fighter Leaders' School at Milfield in Northumberland as an instructor.

He left the RAF in January 1946 with the rank of Squadron Leader, having been awarded a DFC for his two fighter tours.

Gordon Brettell

Brettell began his flying experience in the summer of 1940 on Tiger Moths at 1 EFTS, Hatfield before moving to 5 SFTS, Sealand, where he flew Miles Masters. On completion of his basic and advanced training he made the step up to Spitfires at 58 OTU, Grangemouth, under the expert guidance of Chief Flying Instructor, Wing Commander H.A.V. Hogan, formerly of the RAF's Long-range Development Flight.

Following his time with the 92 'Foot and Mouth', as it was irreverently known, he was promoted to Flight Lieutenant and in 1942 became a Flight Commander with 133 Squadron, one of the three 'Eagle' squadrons made up of US volunteers. On 26 September Brettell led the squadron as escort to B-17 Flying Fortresses of the 97th Bombardment Group who were to attack the Focke-Wulf aircraft plant at Morlaix, near Brest. With a round trip of just under 250 miles the operation should have been straightforward, but the Spitfires flew over a dense overcast and were unaware that they were being blown too far to the south by a northerly jetstream of over 100 mph.

When the rendezvous with the bombers was reached there was no sign of the B-17s who, unknown to Brettell, had arrived 20 minutes early and had already set course for their objective. After wasting precious fuel circling, the Spitfires flew south in pursuit and eventually met up with their charges heading back towards them, having given up any hope of finding the target. More fuel was then wasted as they were forced to zigzag to stay with the bombers and after more than two hours in the air, Brettell led the squadron down through the cloud as by now they should have been approaching the south coast of England. Having descended below the overcast, a coastline was seen with a large town off to the left which was assumed to be Plymouth, but in actual fact was the well defended naval base at Brest.

The German anti-aircraft crews opened up with a formidable barrage and Brettell's aircraft received a direct hit in its starboard wing, causing it to flick into a spin and giving its pilot no chance of baling out. Amazingly he survived the subsequent crash and crawled out of the wreckage with relatively minor injuries. All of 133 Squadron's other Spitfires were either shot down or crash-landed, out of fuel.

After interrogation at *Dulag Luft*, Brettell was sent to *Stalag Luft* III at Sagan, approximately 60 miles SSE of Frankfurt. Here he became heavily involved in the camp's escape organisation, contributing to the intricate work that went into producing forged documentation. By the Spring of 1943 a new compound was nearing completion to the north of the existing accommodation and volunteer prisoners were required to grub up tree roots to clear what would become the parade ground. Recognising the possibilities for escape, Brettell went along. Together with a friend, he hid in the roof of one of the huts at the end of the day's work, while the others in the work party rigged the head count so that their absence went unnoticed. After dark the two got away and in three days made it as far as Stettin on the Baltic coast, only to be recaptured and sent back to endure twenty-one days in solitary confinement.

Almost exactly a year later he took part in the mass breakout on 24 March 1944, an event that was later dramatised in the film *The Great Escape*. Seventy-six prisoners got away before the tunnel was discovered but only three were to make it back to freedom. Of the others, fifty were supposedly 'shot while trying to escape', but in actual fact were murdered on the express orders of Adolf Hitler. Along with three RAF Flight Lieutenants, Romas Marcinkus, Henri Picard and 'Tim' Walenn, Brettell made it as far as Danzig before they were recaptured and handed over to the *Gestapo*. All four men were shot on 29 March 1944.

Tony Cooper

Having joined the RAF Volunteer Reserve in early 1938, Tony Cooper was among the very first intake at 29 E&RFTS, Luton on 1 August where he was taught to fly on Magisters and Hart Trainers. Further training followed on Harts and Audaxes at 9 SFTS, Hullavington in March 1940 and three months later he was commissioned as a Pilot Officer. A naturally gifted pilot, his potential as an instructor was quickly recognised which led to him taking a short course at CFS, Upavon before joining the staff at 7 SFTS, Peterborough.

With the setting up of the Empire Air Training Scheme (later British Commonwealth Air Training Plan) in late 1940, 7 SFTS was one of seven training units that were transferred to Canada where it became 31 SFTS which was based at Kingston, Ontario, and mainly trained

*Flight Lieutenant
Tony Cooper.*
(Cooper)

Fleet Air Arm pilots on Battles, Yales and Harvards. Delays in the training schedule due to weather were rare even though conditions in winter were often severe. The airfield was covered in packed snow and ice for quite lengthy periods and on one occasion Cooper remembers flying at night when the outside air temperature was −40 degrees C! To combat such conditions he wore a specially designed full-face helmet made from chamois leather which he coated with Vaseline jelly on the inside to prevent frostbite. He remained with the unit as an instructor until March 1943 when he was posted back to the UK having been promoted in the meantime to Flight Lieutenant.

Following conversion to the Spitfire at 61 OTU, Rednal, he joined 64 Squadron at Ayr on 7 July 1943 and was to remain with them for the next sixteen months. In early January 1944 he attended a two-week course at the Fighter Leaders' School, Aston Down, which prepared him for future leadership, and shortly after D-Day he duly took over as 'A' Flight Commander having already led the squadron from time to time.

On 27 September 1944, he was flying Spitfire IX MK805 *Peter John III* during an escort of 6 Group heavy bombers to Bottrop when its engine was hit by *flak* over the target. At first the damage did not seem to be too serious, but half way home the Merlin started to run rough and eventually seized. By now the bombers and their escorts had crossed out over the North Sea so Cooper had no choice but to turn back towards the Belgian coast. He was accompanied by Warrant Officer Maunders but as they were flying over a dense overcast, the two were unsure of their exact position. As they entered cloud Maunders lost contact with Cooper due to the slow speed of the latter's aircraft, leaving his leader to carry out a wheels-up landing in a ploughed field near Moerbecke. His luck was in as his Spitfire came down just four miles inside Allied lines, and he was back home and on ops again within 24 hours!

With nearly 170 operational sorties recorded in his logbook, Cooper left 64 Squadron on 6 November 1944, at the end of his tour and spent the next six months at 53 OTU, Kirton-in-Lindsey where he took over as OC 'B' Flight. Following an Instructors' course at the Advanced Gunnery School at Catfoss, he was posted in July 1945 to the Examining Squadron of CFS, Hullavington where he flew many different types of aircraft ranging from B-24 Liberators to Hotspur gliders. His last flight in the RAF took place on 23 October 1945 by which time he had amassed over 2,800 hours flying time, with approximately 800 hours on Spitfires.

On leaving the RAF Tony Cooper returned to his family wholesale food and bakery business in Lowestoft, which supplied provisions to a large part of the town's fishing fleet, eventually taking over as its Managing Director. In the post-war years he remained in contact with a number of his squadron colleagues including his two closest pals, Johnny Plagis and John Harder. Now retired, he lives in Suffolk.

Ian 'Jock' Duncan

Born in the Shettleston area of Glasgow on 21 August 1921, Ian Duncan was educated at the city's Wellshot Academy and worked for a time at Templeton's carpet factory, one of Glasgow's most famous businesses. As his father had served in the RFC during the First World War, he was keen to follow in his footsteps and joined the RAF's Edinburgh Reserve on 24 May 1941. He was eventually called up later that year and his induction into service life took place at Heaton Park near Manchester.

Like many other pilots of the Darlington Spitfire he was taught to fly in Canada and he arrived at 35 EFTS Neepawa, Manitoba on 17 April 1942, to begin basic instruction on Tiger Moths. Four months later he joined Course No. 61 at 14 SFTS Aylmer, Ontario where he flew Harvards as a member of 'E' Flight. Duncan's instructor at Aylmer was Pilot Officer H.W. Collard who would later go on to fly Lancasters at Middleton St George. Collard recalls him as a steady, reliable pilot, and in his opinion would have made an excellent captain of four-engined aircraft, although knowing the ways of the RAF, he was not particularly surprised to discover that he eventually flew Spitfires. Having successfully completed the advanced course, Duncan was among those who organised the Wings Party which took place on 19 November, and was back home in time for Christmas (courtesy of the liner *Queen Elizabeth*).

He continued his training at 17 (P)AFU, Watton on 9 March 1943, where he flew Master IIs, and the following month moved to 61 OTU at Rednal. Here he joined up with Tony Cooper, his future Flight Commander, the two being posted to 64 Squadron within two days of each other. Although kept extremely busy with the demands of squadron life, he managed to visit his family for brief periods during one of which his young sister asked him what it was like to fly a Spitfire. To this day she remembers his answer: 'Oh, it's just like riding a bike, except you don't have to pedal!'

During his eleven months with 64 Squadron Duncan flew fifty-one operational sorties commencing with a convoy patrol on 22 July and was promoted to Flight Sergeant on 21 November. As his experience grew he came to be regarded as an increasingly important member of the squadron and was among the pilots selected for the unit's second patrol over the Omaha beaches on D-Day.

Having flown nine sorties in connection with the Allied invasion, Ian Duncan was killed on 16 June 1944 when his aircraft went out of control after being hit by *flak* near St Lo. At the time of his death Duncan was flying as Tony Cooper's wingman, a position he had taken up on a number of previous operations. Cooper remembers him as being resolute and dependable, and one of the best No. 2s in the squadron. On a personal level his cheerful nature had delighted every-

Sergeant Ian 'Jock' Duncan.
(Mrs M. Grigor)

one he had come into contact with and his loss was mourned not only by 64 Squadron, but by many members of 234 and 611 Squadrons which formed the Deanland Wing.

Ian Duncan is buried in the Bayeux War Cemetery near Calvados in France.

Philip 'Joe' Fargher

From the Isle of Man, Joe Fargher joined 234 Squadron on 21 October 1943 from No. 2 Combat Training Wing to commence a tour that was to be as eventful as any in the late war period. After a relatively quiet start, his adventures began on 14 June 1944 during a beachhead cover patrol between Bayeux and Caen. His aircraft was hit by a burst of 88 mm *flak* which also claimed two other Spitfires flown by Flight Lieutenant Walter Johnston and Flying Officer Bill Painter, all three coming down on an airfield at Coulombs (B.6). Fargher elected to lower the undercarriage during his approach but had the misfortune to tip up on landing which resulted in a gashed forehead.

The three pilots were given assistance by the Army so that they could return to their unit and eventually stumbled across an airfield where the Commander of the Allied Expeditionary Air Force, Air Chief Marshal

Flight Sergeant 'Joe' Fargher meets Air Chief Marshal Leigh-Mallory.
(Imperial War Museum ref CL129)

Sir Trafford Leigh-Mallory, was about to leave after paying a brief visit. Leigh-Mallory took great interest in their arrival and, aware of the opportunity for a good press story, gave them a lift home in his personal Dakota. As a result of such swift action all three pilots were operational again the following day having featured prominently in the morning edition of a national daily newspaper.

Four weeks later Fargher was in trouble once more when his Spitfire was hit by *flak* during a Rhubarb of the Brest peninsula on 11 July. A glycol leak caused his engine to quickly overheat and he was forced to bale out, a difficult task for someone standing over 6 ft tall. On this occasion his stay in France was a little longer and involved a period with the local *Maquis* who arranged his escape so that he was back in England by the end of the month.

Fargher's luck then held until 9 March 1945, when he was forced to bale out into the North Sea after his Mustang III, FB152, developed engine trouble thirty miles out from the Dutch coast. His position was fixed by his No. 2 who maintained an orbit overhead, and eventually an ASR Warwick arrived on the scene to drop 'Lindholme' survival gear. This unfortunately fell too far away to be of any use and he spent

130

an uncomfortable few hours before finally being retrieved by a rescue launch. As a result of this experience he was able to join the RAF's Caterpillar and Goldfish clubs, which he added to his existing membership of its Escaping Society.

After the war Fargher remained in the RAF and from February 1956 to October 1957 commanded 5 Squadron who were equipped with Venom FB 4s and were based at Wünsdorf in Germany as part of Second Tactical Air Force.

On retirement from the RAF, he transferred to the Middle East where he spent eight years working with the Omani Air Force. He died suddenly in February 1987.

Stan Farmiloe

Stan Farmiloe joined 234 Squadron from No. 2 CTW on the same date as Joe Fargher and flew with them for the rest of the war during which time he completed 101 operational sorties. One of the highlights of his tour was the bombing of the village of Serignac on 29 July 1944, an attack that had been requested by local resistance fighters. The village was evacuated prior to the attack, leaving only the Germans in residence, and the pilots were informed that they could flatten anything except the church, as the arms of the resistance had been hidden in the crypt!

His experiences with the Mustang proved vastly different from those with the Spitfire, and on 9 February 1945 he took part in an operation that 234 Squadron had been planning for some time. The aim was to utilise the long range of the Mustang and fly deep into Germany where they hoped to catch the *Luftwaffe* unawares. Under the operation number 'Rodeo 413', the Mustangs swept as far south as Munich where some four-engined Junkers Ju 290s were spotted dispersed on an airfield. Farmiloe singled out one and fired a two-second burst which produced numerous strikes all over its fuselage.

Shortly afterwards three Arado Ar 96Bs were seen carrying out a practice dogfight at around 5000 ft. Farmiloe quickly latched onto one and followed it as it went into a steep corkscrew dive towards the ground. As they descended through 2000 ft the German pilot appeared to change his mind and pulled up sharply, but this only gave Farmiloe the opportunity to tuck in behind. A two-second burst of fire hit the Arado in its centre section and it went over onto its back, temporarily disappearing from Farmiloe's view. He saw it again just before it crashed in flames on the edge of a large wood. A few moments later he noticed a parachute drifting down which he assumed to be that of his victim. The remaining two enemy aircraft were shot down by other members of the squadron.

On 21 March, Farmiloe was one of three 234 Squadron pilots chosen to escort Mosquitoes during Operation 'Carthage', the famous raid on the Shell Building in Copenhagen which contained the German *Gestapo* headquarters. Although seven aircraft were lost during the attack, it was hailed as a success as over 100 German officers and their Danish accomplices were killed.

Having already flown in the D-Day and Arnhem operations, Farmiloe took part in the final assault of the war by the Airborne Forces when he flew escort during Operation 'Varsity', the crossing of the Rhine, on 24 March 1945, and a month later he flew his longest ever escort sortie (with a flight time of 5 hours 30 minutes) when he accompanied Lancasters as they attacked Hitler's 'Eagles Nest' at Berchtesgaden.

After the war Farmiloe qualified as a Chartered Accountant and also ran a boatyard with his former squadron colleague, Ray Stebbings. Now retired, he lives in Worcestershire.

Gordon Farquharson

As the Darlington Spitfire was leaving Castletown in April 1942 following its landing accident, its pilot, Gordon Farquharson, was also on the move. He had been selected as one of fifty pilots who were to fly Spitfires from the American aircraft carrier USS *Wasp* to Malta, an operation that took place on 9 May 1942 under the code name 'Bowery'.

Having safely completed the long sea crossing, Farquharson joined 126 Squadron and was immediately thrust into a situation not dissimilar to the Battle of Britain of two years before. The island was under daily attack by German and Italian aircraft and in the coming weeks he shot down two, and claimed several others as probably destroyed.

On 15 October, eight aircraft of 126 Squadron were scrambled to intercept an incoming raid but, before they could do so, were bounced by Me 109s. Farquharson's aircraft, BR176, was badly shot about and although he was hit in the foot, he managed to bale out successfully and was pulled from the sea by Malta's much used rescue launch, HSL128.

Two weeks later he was among a number of tour-expired and injured pilots who boarded a Liberator of 511 Squadron, bound for the UK via Gibraltar. The Liberator, AL516, arrived at its refuelling stop in the middle of a bad storm as a result of which it overshot the runway and crashed into the sea. Of the thirty-four passengers, fourteen were killed, and Farquharson, whose foot was still encased in plaster, had to be rescued once again having saved himself by clinging to a piece of floating debris. Other survivors included Wing Commander Arthur Donaldson and Canadian ace, Pilot Officer George 'Screwball' Beurling.

After recovering from his injuries, Farquharson instructed at 61 OTU before commencing his second tour with 416 Squadron on 10 September 1943. Six months later he was still a Pilot Officer, a situation that provoked much sarcastic comment from the Squadron diarist who made a plea to the powers that be to 'get mobile' and promote him to Flying Officer (an upgrading that eventually came through on 26 March 1944).

In May, Farquharson attended an Air Support Training Course at Milfield, but was back in time for D-Day during which he flew two beachhead patrols. Shortly afterwards he had a lucky escape when his Spitfire, MJ787, was hit by *flak*, but he succeeded in bringing it back to base where he carried out a wheels-up landing. His final victory of the war occured on 28 June during a squadron cover patrol around Caen when eight Me 109s were seen diving below. Yellow section used their height advantage to close on the gaggle and Farquharson (Yellow 3) followed one into a climbing turn, firing three two-second bursts which hit the 109 in its forward fuselage, forcing its pilot to take to his parachute.

Having been further promoted to Flight Lieutenant, Farquharson became a Flight Commander for a short period before leaving the squadron on 24 August 1944. Not long after he returned to his native Canada having been awarded a DFC.

David Ferraby

By the time Gordon Farquharson arrived in Malta, David Ferraby had already been on the island for two months, having been among the very first group of pilots to fly Spitfires from HMS *Eagle* during Operation 'Spotter' on 7 March 1942. Joining 249 Squadron, led by former Cranwell cadet Squadron Leader Stan Grant, he was in the thick of things almost immediately and on the 11th, along with the Hurricanes of 185 Squadron, he flew one of four Spitfires which broke up a raid by Ju 88s and Me 109s.

In May 1942, Ferraby joined 185 Squadron which had recently converted onto Spitfires, and on the 14th, flying BR294, he engaged a

Macchi MC 202 which was escorting Ju 88s attacking Takali. The Italian aircraft was severely hit and spun away trailing black smoke but as it was not seen to crash, it could only be claimed as a probable. Just over two weeks later, on 30 May, he added to his score by damaging an Me 109 and sharing in the destruction of a Cant Z.1007 bomber.

On 7 July Ferraby scrambled in AB500 to intercept twelve Ju 88s heading towards Luqa but his No. 2 had to abort his take-off, leaving him in the unenviable position of having to climb alone. Before he could join up with the rest of the squadron he was attacked and hit from behind, flames instantly shooting along the right-hand side of his cockpit. In attempting to bale out, his knees became caught under the rim of the windscreen and he was forced to lower himself back into his burning aircraft to free them. By now his Spitfire was diving vertically at over 400 mph but in his anxiety to get out, his parachute pack snagged on the protruding headrest above his seat. Fortunately he still had plenty of height in hand and on his third attempt he finally broke free, floating down to land in one of Malta's winding lanes with gashed knees and burns to his right leg. Ferraby recalls that he had nothing in the way of protection for his legs as he had taken off wearing shorts and gym shoes!

After his service abroad, he returned to the UK to instruct at 57 OTU, Eshott, but in early July 1943 was given the chance to join 64 Squadron by Johnny Plagis, who he had known in Malta. He remained with the squadron until early 1944 during which time he also attended a two-month fighter-reconnaissance course at 41 OTU, Hawarden flying Mustang Is.

On 16 January 1944 Ferraby was posted to No. 2 Flying Instructors' School at Montrose after which he flew Oxfords with 11 (P)AFU at Calveley and 1524 BAT Flight at Newton. In January 1945 he joined 22 AACU in India where he flew a number of different types ranging from Defiants and Hurricanes to the powerful Vultee Vengeance. Over the coming months the unit flew from several locations including Drigh Road, and in addition to its tasks relating to gunnery practice, it also took on pilot training, Ferraby eventually taking over as Chief Flying Instructor. His final sortie occurred on 31 May 1946 whereupon he retired from the service with the rank of acting Squadron Leader.

Roy Flight

Roy Flight was born in Romford on 6 November 1923 and attended the Royal Liberty School at Gidea Park in Essex. In June 1940, with the

Battle of Britain about to begin, he was keen to join the RAF and presented himself for selection, even though he was still only sixteen years old. Like many before him, he lied about his age and was elated when his deviousness succeeded and he was accepted. However, any visions he had of quickly learning to fly were soon dashed and, much to his disgust, he had to wait almost a year before being called up due to problems with expansion of the training organisation. Even so, he was still three months under-age when he took the controls of a Miles Magister for the first time at 30 EFTS, Burnaston in August 1941.

On completion of the basic course he was informed that the rest of his instruction would take place in Canada and he joined a convoy which sailed from Greenock in mid-October 1941. He recalls that the convoy's Royal Navy escort departed after two days to be replaced by part of the US Fleet, including a battleship and an aircraft carrier. The US warships then carried out 'exercises' around the convoy until it reached St Johns in Newfoundland, an example of the co-operation which existed between Britain and the USA who had yet to enter the war.

Flight completed his advanced flying at 31 SFTS, Kingston, in Ontario (where Tony Cooper was an instructor), before returning to the UK to fly Masters and Hurricanes with 5 (P)AFU at Tern Hill. He then moved to 61 OTU, Rednal where he was to begin a 'love affair' with the Spitfire. Its handling qualities were apparent from his very first flight in one, and he describes it as '... a beautiful, responsive, yet deadly fighter; a joy to fly'. His operational posting came through in September 1942 and was to 118 Squadron with whom he was to fly a total of eighty-six operational sorties .

Before he flew the Darlington Spitfire, Flight's regular aircraft was EP413 which he used to secure his first combat claim on 18 March 1943. Flying as Blue 4 during an escort of Ventura bombers, he attacked a pair of Fw 190s who were about to get onto the tail of Blue 1 (F/L 'Dickie' Newbery) and fired a two-second burst at the leading machine which at once began to stream dense black smoke. The 190 then carried out a series of seemingly uncoordinated manoeuvres before falling into a vertical dive. Flight followed it down but had to break at about 2000 ft when he was set upon by another 190. He easily lost his attacker but nearly misjudged his speed in the dive and pulled out with only 100ft to spare above the sea. Considering his own close call, he felt that the 190 he attacked would have gone straight in and consequently claimed it as probably destroyed.

On 3 May 1943, Roy Flight had an outstanding day which proved that, in the right hands, the Spitfire Vb could be a match for the Focke-Wulf Fw 190 at low level. During an escort of Ventura bombers to Amsterdam, Flight was attacked from behind by a 190 but saw it early and was able to break towards it. Both aircraft fired at each other head on and as he turned to come in from behind, Flight could see that the 190 was on fire below the cockpit. A two-second burst from dead astern at 400 yards caused further damage and prompted the German pilot to bale out, his aircraft crashing five miles NNE of Haarlem.

By now Flight was completely alone and although he flew to within a mile or two of the target, he was unable to locate the rest of the squadron. As he re-crossed the Dutch coast on his way back he was attacked once more from behind by a yellow-nosed Fw 190. After several violent manoeuvres, he managed to turn inside his adversary and fired two short bursts from 250 yards allowing two rings of deflection. He witnessed an explosion near the 190's cockpit and it immediately caught fire and levelled out. A further burst from directly behind caused its undercarriage to sag and it slowly turned over and dived into the sea about five miles from the coast.

Mid-way across the North Sea, Flight came across another Fw 190 attacking two Bostons returning from a raid on Ijmuiden. He dived on it almost vertically but as he had used up all of his 20mm ammunition he was restricted to the use of his four machine-guns. Eventually these too gave out but not before he had noted multiple de Wilde strikes on the 190's wing-roots.

After his bale-out near Merville in the evening of 15 September 1943, Flight was captured and taken prisoner. Although he had pre-pared himself for the possibility of being killed or wounded, he had not entertained any thoughts whatsoever about becoming a PoW and remembers that he was devastated when it occurred. He was eventually sent to *Stalag Luft* III at Sagan where, along with Gordon Brettell, he was involved in 'The Great Escape' but was captured at the tunnel when the breakout was discovered. In February 1945 with the Russians advancing rapidly from the east, many RAF Officers were transferred to *Marlag* und *Milag Nord* near Hamburg where they were to be held as possible hostages. Not long after arriving at the new camp Flight and a friend managed to escape and following various adventures, they joined up with the Guards Armoured Division with whom they remained until they were able to hitch a lift home in an RAF Dakota. Their return to the UK was perfectly timed for them to take part in the VE Day celebrations on 8 May.

Having been disappointed at not being part of the Allied invasion of Europe, Flight was keen to see active service against Japan and got back into practice by flying Harvard IIbs with 5 (P)AFU and Tempest Vs with 56 OTU, before moving onto Spitfire XVIs. By the time he achieved operational status, hostilities in the Pacific had also ceased as a result of which he found that his motivation to be a fighter pilot had gone. He was posted to 695 Squadron at Horsham St Faith for a short period in May 1946 and, appropriately enough, his last flight in the RAF consisted of a fifty-five minute sortie during which he carried out aerobatics in his beloved Spitfire.

On leaving the RAF, he took advantage of the training programmes set up for ex-servicemen and was accepted into Medical School where he qualified as a doctor in 1952. Not long after, he emigrated to New Zealand where he continued in his chosen profession until his retirement. At the time of writing, he lives in Auckland.

Eric Gibbs

By the time that Eric Gibbs flew the Darlington Spitfire he was twenty-nine years of age and considerably older than most of its other pilots. Born on 14 July 1912 in Whittington, Staffordshire, he came to single-engined fighters from the unlikely direction of Coastal Command, where he flew Ansons, Bothas and Blenheims on maritime reconnaissance sorties with 608 (North Riding) Squadron at Thornaby. Commissioned as a Pilot Officer in 1940, he was posted to 54 Squadron at Castletown on 2 January 1942 as 'B' Flight Commander, taking over the squadron three months later.

Gibbs supervised 54 Squadron's transfer to Australia from June-September 1942 where it formed part of No. 1 RAAF Wing at Darwin together with 452 and 457 Squadrons. Having become operational in late January 1943, 54 Squadron's first major action took place on 2 March during an attack on Coomalie which saw the destruction of a Nakajima 'Kate' and two Zero fighters, one of which was shot down by Eric Gibbs.

April was quiet, but on 2 May radar picked up a large enemy formation moving in towards Darwin over the Timor Sea. The squadron's Spitfires were quickly airborne and began their climb to 32,000 ft to get above the attacking force which comprised eighteen Mitsubishi G4M 'Betty' bombers with an escort of twenty-seven Zeros. Having completed their bombing run, the Japanese withdrew over Point Blaze where they were engaged by the defending fighters. Flying a Spitfire Vc,

BS164, Gibbs shot down one of the Zeros, damaged another, and also damaged one of the 'Bettys'.

The next major action took place on 30 June when the USAAF Liberator base at Fenton was attacked. The opposing forces met over Anson Bay and in the subsequent mêlée Gibbs shot down one 'Betty', shared another and claimed two more as damaged. Although the bombers were the main priority he had further success, shooting down one of the Zeros.

Soon after these reversals the Japanese reverted to night bombing and Gibbs' final victory of the war was a 'Betty' shot down on 6 July. Gradually the tide of war turned against Japan so that by the end of 1943 air raids against Darwin had ceased altogether. Gibbs was awarded a DFC in November 1943 and left 54 Squadron in January 1944 on completion of his tour by which time his air combat record stood at 5½ destroyed, plus 5 damaged. After the war he remained in the RAF as a member of its Secretarial Branch and retired from the service in July 1953. It has been recorded that he died in the 1970s.

Bill 'Paddy' Harbison

Described by one of his former squadron colleagues as 'a mad but like-able Irishman', Bill Harbison was educated at Ballymena Academy before joining the RAF in 1941. Following *ab initio* flying on Tiger Moths at 1 EFTS, Hatfield, he completed flight training in Canada and joined 118 Squadron in August 1943. Harbison was to fly with 118 for the rest of the war during which time he was promoted to Flight Lieutenant and led the squadron on a number of occasions. Having converted from Spitfires to Mustang IIIs, his last aerial combat of the war occurred on 23 March 1945 when he damaged an Me 262 jet fighter during a Lancaster escort sortie to Bremen.

After 118 Squadron was disbanded in March 1946, Harbison joined 64 Squadron at Horsham St Faith to fly one of the fastest piston-engined fighters of all time, the de Havilland Hornet. He then moved on to fly Meteors with 263 and 257 Squadrons before commencing a two-year exchange posting with the 1st Fighter Group at March AFB, California, where he became the first serving RAF pilot to fly the super-sonic F-86 Sabre, an aircraft he describes as 'the Spitfire of the jet age'.

In 1950 he was posted to the Central Fighter Establishment at West Raynham and in early 1952 was one of four CFE pilots attached to the USAF in Korea to gain first-hand experience of jet fighter combat. During this period he flew Sabres with the 335th Tactical Fighter

Squadron at Kimpo and took over as team leader following the loss of Wing Commander Johnny Baldwin. On his return he presented a report to CFE on the tactics employed against the MiG-15, and in early 1953 took command of 67 Squadron as they introduced the Sabre to RAF service at Wildenrath in Germany as part of the Second Tactical Air Force.

Following a staff appointment in Air Defence at the MoD, Harbison converted onto the Gloster Javelin at 228 OCU, Leeming before being posted, in January 1958, as CO of 29 Squadron at Acklington. He remained with the squadron until July 1959 during which time it provided all-weather air defence to Northern Britain. Thereafter he crossed the Atlantic and spent three years in Washington, DC working in the Defence section of the British Embassy.

In 1963 he returned to the action with a two-year tour as base commander at Leuchars and presided over its transition from Javelins to Lightnings. In February 1964 the Lightnings of 74 Squadron arrived from Coltishall, and in the following August the resident 23 Squadron also converted onto the new Mach 2 interceptors. Harbison first flew the Lightning at 226 OCU, Middleton St George, and it soon became a particular favourite. He recalls that it was beautiful to fly, handling much better than the F-4 Phantom, and had breathtaking climb performance.

Between 1965 and 1977 Harbison undertook a number of staff duties which culminated in his appointment, in March 1975, as Air Officer Commanding No. 11 Group, Bentley Priory, with responsibility for the Air Defence of the UK, a task he fulfilled until April 1977 when he retired from the RAF with the rank of Air Vice-Marshal. Having been awarded the Air Force Cross in 1956, he was later made a Commander of the Order of the British Empire, and in 1977 became a companion of the Order of the Bath.

After leaving the RAF, Harbison returned to the USA where he represented British Aerospace's military aircraft interests as Vice-President, Special Aircraft Programmes. He remains a consultant to the company and lives in Virginia.

John 'Junior' Harder

John Harder was born on 18 July 1923 in New York and educated at St Mark's School and Southboro College, Massachusetts, before joining the RAF in 1941 at the age of eighteen. Following his own country's entry into the war he chose to stay in the service, unlike many of his fellow Americans who transferred to the USAAF as soon as they were allowed.

Harder joined 64 Squadron on 24 February 1943 from 58 OTU and his potential as a future leader was quickly recognised. He also possessed excellent technical knowledge which was to prove to be a considerable asset to the squadron. Slim, and with boyish good looks, he was soon given the nickname 'Junior' which led to his own personal emblem being painted on the cowling of his regular aircraft, that of a baby wearing a nappy. As pilot of the Darlington Spitfire, he was introduced to readers of the *Northern Despatch* in December 1943, although the otherwise accurate report referred to him as Flying Officer 'Harding'. In it he was quoted as saying that he was anxious to have a look at the town which had given his 'kite' its name.

A week after he was rescued from the North Sea (see page 78), Harder attended a three week course at the Fighter Leaders' School at Milfield, subsequently taking over as the squadron's 'B' Flight Commander. Not long after, on 24 July 1944, he was flying Spitfire IX, MK258, when it was badly damaged by *flak* during a patrol of the Aron area, to the east of Mayenne. Although he managed to bale out of his stricken aircraft successfully, his parachute failed to deploy fully and his descent was much too rapid. He was fortunate to come down in some trees which broke his fall, but in the process he suffered severe back injuries. Harder was eventually discovered by a local farmer and his wife who took him to their home where he then began a slow and painful recovery under the care of a local doctor.

During the early part of his convalescence he vowed to himself that he would leave as soon as he could as his French hosts were putting their lives at considerable risk by harbouring him. This he did after two months but, as he was still not fully fit, he was captured and spent the rest of the war as a prisoner, initially at *Stalagluft* III and later at *Stalag* III, a *Wehrmacht* camp about 30 km SE of Berlin. At the end of the war, as German resistance crumbled, the country slid into chaos and confusion as millions fled in front of the invading Russian army. Aware of the dangers, Harder preferred to dictate his own repatriation arrangements which he felt afterwards to have been the right decision. Many he had known in the prison camp were led away by the Russians, supposedly to freedom, but he did not see them again and he feared for their safety.

In the post-war years, he began a career in civil aviation which saw him fly most of the major American airliners up to and including the Boeing 747. He was President and Director of Flight Operations at

Starflite Inc of White Plains, New York from 1957–1966, and was also Senior Captain. The airline operated a wide variety of aircraft from Beech 18 to Lockheed L.1649A Starliner and offered domestic and international contract services to major American Corporations from its Westchester base. In addition Harder flew many famous entertainers in his aircraft including Frank Sinatra and Bob Hope. After a year as Director of Corporate Development at Kaman Aircraft Corporation, he took an instructor's post with the Boeing Company in Seattle, a task that he carried out until 1973. His final work in aviation took him all over the world as he advised on air crash investigations, a task for which his technical expertise was ideally suited.

Shortly before his death in the late 1970s, Harder was invited to revisit the village in France where he had been shot down in 1944. He met many of those who had helped him evade the Germans and was given his old parachute which had been signed by all the villagers. The lady who made the presentation apologised that several panels were missing as she had used them to make her daughter's wedding dress!

Walter 'Johnnie' Johnston

Although Walter Johnston did not fly the Darlington Spitfire, he is unique in its history as the only pilot to have served in two squadrons (92 and 234) at the same time as the aircraft itself. To precis Johnston's wartime flying career is extremely difficult as his experiences would in themselves be sufficient to fill a book. In an RAF career dating back to 1938, he accumulated over 2000 flying hours, a figure which includes approximately 1000 hours on Spitfires, with over 500 hours on operations. During that time he survived a mid-air fire in a Hawker Audax, three crash landings, and was credited with the destruction of four enemy aircraft.

His first tour commenced in late 1940 with 152 Squadron at Warmwell flying Spitfire Is, but these were soon exchanged for Mark IIs and in April 1941 he moved with the squadron to Portreath in Cornwall. Here they received long range Mark IIs, an aircraft that Johnston describes as 'awful' due to adverse handling characteristics brought about by its asymmetric overload tank.

In July 1941 he was posted to 92 Squadron and on 27 September destroyed two Me 109s during a sweep that was followed by the Prime Minister, Winston Churchill, in the ops room at Biggin Hill. Johnston had called the squadron to break in a typically loud and abusive manner and as his expletives blasted out of the Tannoy there had been

Flight Lieutenant Walter 'Johnnie' Johnston (right) stands with Flight Sergeant 'Joe' Fargher and Flying Officer Bill Painter beside Leigh-Mallory's personal Dakota. Sadly, Painter was killed three days after this photograph was taken. (via Johnston)

concern from many as to the PM's reaction. When Churchill met the pilots afterwards however, he merely smiled and said '… and you must be "Johnnie", the Geordie with the fine flow of language!'

In December 1941 he began his rest period with 61 OTU where one of his trainees was the future French ace, Pierre Clostermann. During this time Johnston also attended Central Flying School, Upavon, and the Central Gunnery School, Sutton Bridge, where he qualified for both Flying and Weapons instruction. He moved to CGS as an instructor in March 1943 where he also became involved in testing early versions of the gyro gunsight, a device that was generally referred to at the time as 'Wandering Willie', due to the apparent aimless movement of the sighting graticule. After six months he left to commence his second operational tour, joining 234 Squadron.

142

On 14 June 1944 he was flying BL415 on a beachhead cover patrol when it was hit by the same burst of *flak* that claimed 'Joe' Fargher's Spitfire. His aircraft was lifted 200 ft upwards by the blast, its starboard wingtip clipped by a further two feet. A second burst then loosened the access panels covering the engine which blew back, damaging the hood to such an extent that Johnston was unable to bale out. Control was marginal, but by holding full port aileron he found that it was possible to keep the wings level which allowed some degree of manoeuvre by the use of rudder. The subsequent crash landing at around 200 mph destroyed much of what remained of his Spitfire but, despite all the odds, he was pulled from the wreckage apparently uninjured and was flying again the next day.

Johnston remained with 234 until November 1944 when he was promoted to Squadron Leader prior to taking over as Sector Gunnery Officer at Manston. His final post in the RAF was as Chief Flying Instructor with No. 1330 Conversion Unit at Bilbeis in Egypt, converting pilots onto a number of American multi-engined types, including Dakotas, Mitchells and Liberators, so that they could be ferried back to the UK. Although still a Squadron Leader, he took over as base commander during which time the station played an important part in the so-called 'Meeting of Kings' to determine future Middle East policy. Johnston left the RAF in 1946 but continued to fly Tiger Moths and Chipmunks with the Volunteer Reserve until 1959.

His high speed crash landing in 1944 eventually caused difficulties and in the post-war years he began to suffer from back problems which eventually led to his early retirement. Having spent many years living in Yorkshire, he now lives in Cornwall.

Don Kingaby

After his rest period at 58 OTU, Grangemouth, Kingaby returned to operations with 111 Squadron at Debden in March 1942, but within a month had been transferred to 64 Squadron, which was based at Hornchurch and equipped with Spitfire Vbs. In June the squadron introduced the much improved Spitfire IX into RAF service and it was not long before Kingaby was adding to his score with the destruction of an Fw 190 on 30 July.

There followed a series of rapid promotions which saw him become a Flight Commander with 64 Squadron for a short period, before taking over command of 122 Squadron with the rank of Squadron Leader. Thanks to the enlightened attitude displayed by both Jamie

*Wing Commander
Don Kingaby DSO
DFM**.*
(Imperial War Museum
ref CH13615)

*Wing Commander
Don Kingaby DSO
DFM**.*
(Imperial War Museum
ref CH13615)

Rankin and 'Dickie' Milne, his former COs at 92 Squadron, he had gained considerable leadership experience in the earlier part of his career and he used it to great effect with his new squadron. A firm believer in leading by example, Kingaby showed the way in January 1943 with the destruction of two German fighters in two days which led to further recognition and the award of a Distinguished Service Order (DSO).

Kingaby became tour-expired in May 1943 after which he spent a year at Fighter Command HQ, Bentley Priory, on a staff appointment. Following his brief return to operations around the time of D-Day, his air-fighting skills were utilised at the Advanced Gunnery School at Catfoss, where he worked under his former Wing Leader, 'Sailor'

Malan, and by the end of the war he had been further decorated with the award of an American DFC and a Belgian *Croix de Guerre*. Throughout his operational career he flew over 300 sorties, and his only combat injury was a damaged finger sustained during a low-level strafing attack by Me 109s back in 1940! He was officially credited with the destruction of 22½ enemy aircraft, 6 probably destroyed, and 11 damaged.

Although the following words were appended to his logbook as he left 92 Squadron, they would have been equally appropriate at the end of his wartime service:

> 'Kingaby has proved himself one of the most brilliant fighter pilots of this war. His keenness to engage the enemy and his courage and resource in action are of the highest order.' – Flight Lieutenant J.H. Sanderson O.C. 'B' Flight 92 Squadron.

Having been awarded a permanent commission, he remained in the RAF and from February 1949 to April 1952 commanded 72 Squadron during which time he led their Vampire aerobatic team who were the first to roll seven aircraft in line abreast. Another honour was bestowed in 1952 when he received the Air Force Cross.

Kingaby retired from the RAF in 1958 with the rank of Wing Commander and he spent his last years in the USA, to where he and his wife Helen had emigrated to join their two daughters. He died there in December 1990 after suffering a long illness.

Ron 'Joe' May

Ron May was born in Yarram, Victoria on 11 November 1922 and joined the Royal Australian Air Force Reserve in April 1941 at the age of eighteen. His long journey towards operational flying took him to training camps in Egypt and South Africa, and then basic flying training on Tiger Moths at 25 EFTS, Belvedere in Southern Rhodesia. Having taken the advanced course at 20 SFTS, Cranbourne, he finally arrived in the UK in early December 1942, but then had to undergo refresher flying at 22 EFTS, Cambridge, and 17 (P)AFU, Watton, where he became accustomed to flying in typical British weather. His first flight in a Spitfire took place at 53 OTU, Kirton-in-Lindsey, and with the rank of Flight Sergeant, he joined 234 Squadron at Hutton Cranswick on 21 October 1943.

On 17 April 1944, May was taking part in a reconnaissance over the Brest peninsula when his Spitfire, W3822, was hit by *flak* which

Pilot Officer Ron 'Joe' May. (Stebbings)

damaged the starboard wing and blew a one foot square hole in the fin and rudder. Control became extremely difficult, especially in the yawing plane, but he managed to return safely, the Squadron ORB praising him for a 'fine job' in saving his aircraft. Such first-rate airmanship did not go unnoticed, and the following month he was promoted to Pilot Officer.

Five months later, on 14 October, May was flying Mustang III, FB215 as escort to a raid by over 1000 heavy bombers on Duisburg, when engine problems caused him to carry out a forced landing on a disused airfield near Moerbecke in Belgium. When committed to landing, he realised that the strip was too short and, worse still, was obstructed by a pile of gravel at its end. His Mustang, which carried the AZ-Y codes previously worn by the Darlington Spitfire, was written off in the ensuing crash, but May was uninjured and was able to rejoin his squadron after help from local resistance forces. Coincidentally, his aircraft came down not far from where Tony Cooper had force landed just three weeks before.

May remained with 234 Squadron until 1 May 1945 during which time he had the pleasure of shooting up Göring's yacht, and on another occasion, flew under Tower Bridge for a dare. Not surprisingly, the latter incident does not feature in his logbook, or any other official documentation! Like Stan Farmiloe, he also took part in the raid on the *Gestapo* headquarters situated in the Shell Building in Copenhagen.

Having been discharged from the RAAF in November 1945 with the rank of Flying Officer, May returned to Australia but maintained his piloting skills by instructing on Tiger Moths and Avrotrainers at Yarram until November 1950. Thereafter most of his time was given over to farming, in particular his large herd of dairy and beef cattle which he managed until his death in January 1995 at the age of seventy-two.

Scott Morrison

Although he was to fly Spitfires for two years at the end of the war, Scott Morrison's initial contribution to the war effort was very much ground based. At the tender age of sixteen, he joined the 39th entry at No. 1 School of Technical Training at Halton in January 1939, and after successfully completing the course, was posted to Jurby in the Isle of Man in early 1941. A year later he was delighted to be given the opportunity to re-muster for flying training and undertook elementary tuition on Tiger Moths at 10 EFTS, Stoke Orchard in Gloucestershire.

Having proved his aptitude for flying, Morrison sailed to Halifax in Nova Scotia aboard the *Letitia*, before commencing further training at 3 BFTS Miami in Oklahoma where he flew the Fairchild PT-19, Vultee BT-13 and AT-6 Texan. The basic and advanced courses took six months to complete so that by February 1943 he was sailing home again (this time on the liner *Queen Elizabeth*) although as he had to share his cabin with seven others, there was little in the way of luxury! Back in the UK he flew Miles Masters at 5 (P)AFU, Tern Hill, before moving onto Spitfires at 53 OTU, Kirton-in-Lindsey, where his flying was graded as 'Exceptional'.

Morrison joined 64 Squadron on 22 February 1944 and during the next ten months flew sixty-six operational sorties (including five trips in the Darlington Spitfire). His busiest time occurred in the two-week period after D-Day when he took part in fourteen cover patrols over the Utah and Omaha beachheads. The squadron moved from Harrowbeer to Bradwell Bay on the last day in August 1944 and the following morning Morrison took off in Spitfire IX MK775 for a sweep over north-eastern France. Flying as Birdie Blue 3, a large truck convoy was located near Lille, one that was able to look after itself better than most as he recalls:

'Each section of four aircraft attacked individually but, unknown to us, some of the trucks had 20 mm anti-aircraft guns mounted inside them. Whilst attacking the convoy a shell exploded immediately underneath my Spitfire and pieces of shrapnel pierced its radiators. I pulled the aircraft out of the action and then, noticing a slight loss of coolant, quickly decided to fly directly to the coast at Dunkirk, this being my most direct route home. My thinking was to get as far across the Channel as I could and then bale out, although I had a feeling that my engine would not be able to take me that far. I could see a jagged hole in each wing and was accompanied by Flight Sergeant Scott who was keeping an eye open for the first sign of smoke.

'I flew on at about 2,500–3,000 ft but when within sight of the coast-line, my engine began to smoke. Scott advised me to bale out but the canopy would not open, perhaps it had been damaged by the anti-aircraft fire. Looking around for an area to land, I chose a long narrow field and proceeded to crash-land my Spitfire, wheels up! I did this with a heavy heart as the aircraft had been allocated for my exclusive use on August 10, 1944.

'After much difficulty, I finally opened the canopy and located the self-destruct incendiary device, but the strike unit would not operate. A young French boy and his sister then approached and spoke in English – "The Germans are near". They tore off my pilots badge and my Flight Sergeant's stripes and pointing, said in French – "*Boche par la, allez vite!*" Thanking them, I did as advised and crouching very low along various ditches, came upon some women working in a field. With the little French at my disposal I asked them for directions to the south. Continuing along ditches, I came to a main road along which many Germans moved on foot and in vehicles. I crossed at an opportune moment.

'Choosing a farm a bit off the beaten track, I found the farmer and did a deal. In exchange for my watch, he gave me an old jacket, a hat, a pitch-fork, and a sack full of hay. It was now about two in the afternoon and feeling more French than Scottish I headed south and was able to use my button compass which I had removed from my old tunic. I kept to paths along the fields, keeping away from roads. When the odd person spoke, I just answered "*Bonjour*". At last, late in the afternoon, I saw a blond haired youth working in a field adjoining a big farm. Thinking he may be

German, I made sure that my escape knife was handy just in case, but he was the farmer's son, Andre Duyck. On taking me to the front door of the farmhouse, I then met his mother who spoke English (British soldiers had been billeted at her parents' house during the 1914–18 war), Andre's father and his younger sister Paulette.

'As many Germans were in the vicinity, I was shown a hiding place on top of a large cupboard in their kitchen. Andre and Paulette helped to raise the alarm when, on three occasions, the Germans arrived, not looking for me, but for methods of transport to help them escape from the Allied armies spreading out from the invasion beachhead. After nine days we were discovered by a Canadian Army column and then the reconnaissance group of a forward unit arrived to be billeted at the farm. On the evening prior to my departure, Mr Duyck made an excavation in his garden and produced many bottles of wine and a happy party took place.

'The next day, on an Army motorbike, I headed southward and eventually stopped at St Omer (out of petrol). I then scrounged a lift on an ambulance, in return for helping with the general duties, but at the Normandy beachhead there was no air transport available back to England. I was then taken to Paris in an Army 3-tonner and eventually flown out of Le Bourget in an Anson back to an aerodrome near Portsmouth. I finally arrived at Fighter Command headquarters for debriefing – having been interrogated for 1½ hours and answering all questions satisfactorily, I was sent on one week's survivor's leave and one week's disembarkation leave. I returned to my squadron on October 2, 1944 to resume operations.'

Morrison was posted to 132 Squadron on 17 November 1944 and soon after sailed for the Far East. With his new squadron, he flew Spitfire LF VIIIs from Vavuyina in Ceylon until May 1945, before transferring to Madura in southern India where he converted onto the Griffon-engined Spitfire XIV. Not long after a further move took place to Kai Tak, Hong Kong, where the squadron remained until it was disbanded on 15 April 1946, although by this time Morrison had already been demobbed and had sailed for home aboard HMS *Reaper*. During his two years' active service Morrison was commissioned and left the RAF with the rank of Flying Officer.

Ray Stebbings

A qualified pharmacist, Ray Stebbings was called up for RAF service in August 1941 and soon found himself aboard HMS *Pasteur* bound for Canada, his first step on the way to learning to fly. Although vast numbers of aircrew were trained in Canada, Stebbings was heading much further south, to Alabama in the USA. As America had not yet entered the war, to avoid internment in a neutral country, trainees had to cross the border devoid of all signs of rank, a convenient solution to a tricky problem and one that suited both countries nicely.

Stebbings began his elementary flying training on the Stearman PT-17 at Hargrove Van de Graaff Field near Tuscaloosa before moving up to the more advanced Vultee BT-13 Valiant at Gunter Field, Montgomery, and the AT-6 Texan at Maxwell Field. After passing out, he was given the opportunity to remain in the USA as an instructor and took a course at Flying Instructors' School, before returning to Gunter Field to take up his new duties. For the next nine months he taught USAAC cadets to fly before being posted back to the UK in April 1943.

After his return he underwent a period of refresher training which included flying Master IIs and Hurricane Is at 7(P)AFU, Peterborough, and Spitfire Is and IIs at 57 OTU, Eshott. As a result his operational debut was postponed until July 1944 when he joined 234 Squadron at Predannack.

Stebbings remained with 234 until 15 January 1945 when he flew as escort to Lancasters of 3 Group during an operation to attack a benzol plant at Bochum. During the withdrawal phase his Mustang, FB222 'Orange 2', was hit from behind by a similar machine of 19 Squadron, breaking it in two aft of the cockpit. The following extract comes from his book *All For A Caterpillar*:

'The collision took place as I heaved on the stick. I was thrown violently about in the cockpit and received a hard knock on the head, losing my senses rapidly. I could not stop the plane from tumbling and spinning hopelessly out of control and the cockpit controls were useless. I tried to pull myself together during what seemed like ages, but must have been a matter of seconds. I managed to reach over and yank the hood emergency release (the red handle on the starboard side of the canopy).

'Centrifugal force was hurling me outwards and the hood caught me on the head, cutting open my eyebrow, and ripping off my helmet. Fortunately it probably disconnected my oxygen and radio leads as well. I fumbled for the safety straps and then realised I was falling through cold space. I could see absolutely nothing! In this same second I was tearing at my harness for the parachute release which I must have operated

*Flight Lieutenant
Ray Stebbings.*
(Halloran)

successfully because I was jerked out of my dreams by a sickening thud as the straps tightened around my legs.'

Stebbings descended through thick cloud and landed in snow near the small German town of Issum. As well as suffering a head injury, he had also hurt his leg which meant that he was unable to move very far from the crash site and was soon captured. There followed twenty-four days in solitary confinement at *Dulag Luft*, Oberursel, before transfer to PoW camp at *Oflag* III near Nuremberg. Here Stebbings kept busy running the internal affairs for the camp, together with an American Major, but his most anxious time came at the very end of the war when the prisoners were subjected to a sixteen-day forced march through Bavaria to *Stalag* VIIa at Moosburg where, it was rumoured, they were to be held as hostage. Within two weeks however, Patton's 3rd Army broke through in the area and liberation came on 29 April 1945.

After the war Stebbings returned to his chosen profession, but in later years became the Director of several commercial enterprises, including a fast food chain and a company making antique reproduction furniture. His love of flying continued in the post-war years and he acquired a private pilot's licence which he maintained until 1975. For many years he was Honorary Secretary of the 234 Squadron Association. Even now, at the age of eighty-two, he still indulges his passion for flying by occasionally taking the controls of a Stearman biplane, the type in which he first took to the air back in 1941.

Ian Walker

Born in Glasgow on 20 November 1920, Ian Walker served in the Army from April 1939 until his transfer to the RAF as an Aircraftsman 2nd Class in July 1941. Having been remustered as an Airman Pilot in October 1942, he eventually joined 611 Squadron as a Sergeant pilot in October 1943 and served with them for nearly two years during which time he was promoted to Flying Officer and became a deputy Flight Commander.

In early October 1944 the squadron moved to Skaebrae in the Orkney Islands, with 'A' Flight detached further north still at Sumburgh in the Shetlands. Normally a quiet backwater, it was anything but in the early hours of 9 October as Walker was scrambled in BS282, together with another Spitfire, to intercept an unidentified aircraft. His logbook comments describe what happened next:

> 'First scramble from Sumburgh. Intercepted "Weather Willie" midway between island and Norwegian coast. With Kenny Mack's aid, shot him up, leaving him to ditch in flames. Shared this fun and games with crew of five Huns last seen having a spot of trouble with their dinghy drill. Claim one Junkers Ju 88 destroyed!'

Before returning to base Walker climbed to 8000 ft to transmit for a radio fix and the German crew were seen once again by an ASR Anson just before nightfall. As there were no ships in the area there was little that could be done to assist the airmen and the chances of them surviving the night were extremely slim. The following day Walker's exploits were featured by the newspapers who described the long-distance interception as the 'perfect kill'.

The squadron moved south again to Hawkinge in December 1944 and shortly afterwards converted onto Mustang IVs. On 16 April 1945, Walker flew KH743 as 'White 3' during Ramrod 1542, the escort of eighteen Lancasters of 617 Squadron who dropped 12,000 lb 'Tallboy' bombs to destroy the pocket-battleship *Lutzow* at Swinemunde. The squadron's Mustangs then flew on to sweep the area around Berlin where they became the first RAF pilots to meet up with their Russian counterparts when they encountered a number of Il-2 Shturmoviks escorted by Yak fighters. Shortly afterwards 611 engaged a large gaggle of Fw 190s and shot down six without loss, one of which fell to the guns of Ian Walker

His last operational sortie took place on 25 April during which he flew escort to the Bomber Command attack on Berchtesgaden. By the end of the war he had flown 800 hours, of which more than 200 hours were operational.

Walker remained with 611 Squadron until August 1945 and was mentioned in Despatches for his distinguished service. Post-war, he was granted a commission as a Flying Officer in the reconstituted RAF Volunteer Reserve, a post he held until June 1952.

Appendix A

Squadrons and Bases

Squadron	Base	Period
92	Biggin Hill	12/07/41 –25/09/41
	Gravesend	25/09/41 –20/10/41
54	Castletown	01/03/42 – 19/04/42
118	Coltishall	08/07/43 – 15/08/43
	Westhampnett	15/08/43 – 24/08/43
	Merston	24/08/43 – 19/09/43
64	West Malling	19/09/43 – 25/09/43
	Coltishall	25/09/43 – 21/01/44
	Ayr	21/01/44 – 03/02/44
	Coltishall	03/02/44 – 29/04/44
	Deanland	29/04/44 – 23/06/44
	Harrowbeer	23/06/44 – 03/07/44
611	Predannack	03/07/44 – 12/07/44
234	Predannack	12/07/44 – 28/08/44
	North Weald	28/08/44 – 05/10/44
63	North Weald	05/10/44 – 28/10/44

Appendix B

Combat Claims

Date	Pilot	Squadron	Destroyed	Probable	Damaged
07/08/41	F/Sgt D.E.Kingaby	92	-	1	1
09/08/41	F/Sgt D.E.Kingaby	92	1	1	-
01/10/41	F/Sgt D.E.Kingaby	92	1	1	-
03/10/41	F/Sgt D.E.Kingaby	92	1	-	-
27/07/43	P/O R.J.Flight	118	$\frac{1}{2}$	-	-
		TOTAL	$3\frac{1}{2}$	3	1

Claims by F/Sgt D.E.Kingaby – Messerschmitt Me 109F
Claim by P/O R.J.Flight – Messerschmitt Me 109G (Shared with F/O C.L.F. Talalla).

Appendix C

Pilots

Squadron	Pilot	Operations	Remarks
92	P/O P.H.Beake	2	see chapter 11
	P/O G.E.Brettell	8	see chapter 11
	P/O E.A.G.C.Bruce	2	Later F/O 185 Sqn
	Sgt G.P.Hickman	1	PoW 20/9/41
	F/Sgt D.E.Kingaby	37	see chapter 11
	F/L J.W.Lund	1	KIA 2/10/41
	P/O E.W.H.Phillips	1	KIA 26/8/41
54	F/Sgt G.H.T Farquharson	3	see chapter 11
	F/L E.M.Gibbs	1	see chapter 11
	Sgt Varney	1	
118	F/L A.Drew	7	Later S/L 118 Sqn 3/45–3/46
	F/O P.S.Dunning	2	
	P/O R.J.Flight	26	see chapter 11
	P/O W.Harbison	1	see chapter 11
	Sgt J.Jones	3	
	F/Sgt N.K.Paull	1	
	Sgt F.L.Spencer	2	
64	F/L E.Andrews	2	see chapter 11
	F/O W.Bilsland	1	
	F/O K.V.Calder	2	
	F/L A.G.H.Cooper	5	see chapter 11
	P/O G.C.Coupar	1	
	P/O N.J. de Verteuil	4	
	F/Sgt J.D.M.Duncan	23	see chapter 11
	F/O D.L.Ferraby	2	see chapter 11
	F/O J.W.Harder	8	see chapter 11
	F/Sgt G.R.Maunders	2	
	F/O H.J.Meharry	1	KIA 5/8/44
	F/Sgt W.S.Morrison	5	
	Lt J.Muzard	1	
	F/O J.B.Ormerod	1	
	F/O W.A.Smart	2	KIA 3/7/44
	F/O D.A.B.Smiley	2	
	F/Sgt F.Swadling	1	
	F/O A.T.Thorpe	1	

Pilots

	F/Sgt A.Travis	1	
	F/Sgt R.A.L.Williams	1	
611	W/O D.L.McNeil	1	
	F/Sgt I.G.Walker	3	see chapter 11
234	F/L T.W.Berry	3	
	F/Sgt A.C.Butler	2	
	F/Sgt J.W.Crowhurst	2	
	F/Sgt S.T.Farmiloe	7	see chapter 11
	F/Sgt T.P.Fargher	2	see chapter 11
	F/O R.H.Harry	1	
	P/O S.C.Halloran	2	
	P/O J.R.May	12	see chapter 11
	F/Sgt A.Morgan	8	
	F/O R.D.Stebbings	2	see chapter 11
63	F/L J.D.Scholey	2	

Operations Log

Date	Pilot	Operation	Flight times	Duration
92 Squadron				
20/07/41	Kingaby	Sweep	2200–2230	0.30
21/07/41	Kingaby	Sweep	0740–0915	1.35
21/07/41	Kingaby	Sweep	1915–2100	1.45
22/07/41	Kingaby	Weather Recce	0745–0840	0.55
22/07/41	Kingaby	Sweep	1235–1400	1.25
23/07/41	Kingaby	Sweep	1235–1355	1.20
23/07/41	Kingaby	Sweep	1935–2100	1.25
24/07/41	Kingaby	Sweep	1125–1300	1.35
24/07/41	Beake	Sweep	1355–1520	1.25
24/07/41	Lund	ASR	1720–1920	2.00
25/07/41	Beake	Convoy Patrol	0755–0915	1.20
03/08/41	Phillips	Rhubarb	1735–1830	0.55
05/08/41	Kingaby	Patrol–Canterbury	1320–1400	0.40
06/08/41	Kingaby	Sweep	1835–1935	1.00
07/08/41	Kingaby	Sweep	1030–1200	1.30
07/08/41	Kingaby	Sweep	1650–1830	1.40
09/08/41	Kingaby	Sweep	1720–1850	1.30
10/08/41	Kingaby	Sweep	1245–1405	1.20
12/08/41	Kingaby	Sweep	1100–1245	1.45
12/08/41	Kingaby	Sweep	1730–1855	1.25
14/08/41	Kingaby	Sweep/Escort	1345–1445	1.00
14/08/41	Kingaby	Sweep	1640–1810	1.30
16/08/41	Kingaby	Sweep	0725–0910	1.45
16/08/41	Kingaby	Sweep	1210–1330	1.20
16/08/41	Kingaby	Sweep	1735–1855	1.20
18/08/41	Bruce	Sweep	1405–1550	1.45
18/08/41	Bruce	Sweep	1730–1900	1.30
19/08/41	Kingaby	Sweep	1020–1155	1.35
19/08/41	Kingaby	Sweep	1530–1645	1.15
19/08/41	Kingaby	Sweep	1800–1925	1.25
21/08/41	Kingaby	Sweep	0835–1000	1.25
22/08/41	Kingaby	Sweep-aborted (R/T failure)	–	0.10
26/08/41	Brettell	Sweep	1740–1905	1.25
27/08/41	Brettell	Sweep	0620–0800	1.40

27/08/41	Brettell	Scramble Hawkinge	1030–1210	1.40
27/08/41	Brettell	Rhubarb (scrubbed)	1635–1645	0.10
29/08/41	Brettell	Sweep	0630–0825	1.55
30/08/41	Brettell	Convoy Patrol	1010–1200	1.50
31/08/41	Brettell	Sweep	0730–0915	1.45
31/08/41	Hickman	Sweep	1130–1315	1.45
31/08/41	Brettell	Convoy Patrol	1815–2005	1.50
18/09/41	Kingaby	Sweep	1405–1455	0.50
20/09/41	Kingaby	Sweep	1440–1610	1.30
21/09/41	Kingaby	Sweep	1515–1700	1.45
30/09/41	Kingaby	Rhubarb	1510–1550	0.40
01/10/41	Kingaby	Sweep	1130–1310	1.40
01/10/41	Kingaby	Sweep	1530–1640	1.10
03/10/41	Kingaby	Sweep	1330–1525	1.55
13/10/41	Kingaby	Sweep	1320–1510	1.50
15/10/41	Kingaby	Patrol Manston	0710–0820	1.10
15/10/41	Kingaby	Patrol (scrubbed)	1510–1515	0.05
16/10/41	Kingaby	Rhubarb	1105–1230	1.25

54 Squadron

23/03/42	Farqu-harson	Patrol	0825–0940	1.15
26/03/42	Farqu-harson	Scramble	1110–1145	0.35
01/04/42	Varney	Convoy Patrol	1525–1645	1.20
01/04/42	Gibbs	Convoy Patrol	1725–1845	1.20
01/04/42	Farqu-harson	Convoy Patrol	1910–2015	1.05

118 Squadron

09/07/43	Flight	Distil	0935–1105	1.30
18/07/43	Flight	Beaufighter Escort	1425–1550	1.25
18/07/43	Flight	Beaufighter Escort	1955–2130	1.35
19/07/43	Flight	Roadstead	1405–1545	1.40
24/07/43	Flight	Shipping Recce	1020–1150	1.30
25/07/43	Flight	Mitchell Escort	1410–1555	1.45
25/07/43	Flight	Boston Escort	1910–2035	1.25
26/07/43	Flight	Shipping Recce	1025–1150	1.25
27/07/43	Flight	Mitchell Escort	1920–2150	1.30
28/07/43	Flight	Marauder Escort	1005–1205	2.00
28/07/43	Flight	Shipping Recce	2000–2115	1.15
29/07/43	Flight	Marauder Escort	0940–1110	1.30
29/07/43	Flight	Marauder Escort	1750–1920	1.30
30/07/43	Flight	Boston Escort	1000–1140	1.40

06/08/43	Dunning	Shipping Recce	0630–0755	1.25
06/08/43	Flight	ASR	1825–2015	1.50
06/08/43	Jones	ASR	2120–2300	1.40
11/08/43	Flight	Shipping Recce	0635–0745	1.10
12/08/43	Jones	Marauder Escort	1005–1135	1.30
13/08/43	Flight	Beaufighter Escort	1045–1220	1.35
15/08/43	Flight	Marauder Escort	0950–1115	1.25
16/08/43	Flight	Marauder Escort	1610–1745	1.35
18/08/43	Jones	Marauder Escort	1000–1150	1.50
19/08/43	Drew	Marauder Escort	1125–1300	1.35
22/08/43	Spencer	Marauder Escort	1750–1845	0.55
23/08/43	Paull	Marauder Escort	0735–0835	1.00
30/08/43	Dunning	Ventura Escort	1810–1945	1.35
31/08/43	Flight	Mitchell Escort	0730–0905	1.35
05/09/43	Flight	Boston Escort	0825–1035	2.10
06/09/43	Flight	Marauder Escort	0645–0820	1.35
06/09/43	Drew	Marauder Escort	1705–1845	1.40
07/09/43	Drew	Marauder Escort	0755–0940	1.45
08/09/43	Flight	Mitchell Escort	0920–1110	1.50
09/09/43	Drew	Convoy Patrol	0550–0745	1.55
09/09/43	Flight	Convoy Patrol	0810–0950	1.40
09/09/43	Drew	Boston Escort	1355–1525	1.30
11/09/43	Flight	Marauder Escort	1655–1840	1.45
13/09/43	Flight	Sweep	1800–1930	1.30
15/09/43	Drew	Marauder Escort	1710–1845	1.35
18/09/43	Spencer	Marauder Escort	0950–1140	1.50
18/09/43	Drew	Weather Recce	1410–1505	0.55
18/09/43	Harbison	Marauder Escort	1630–1730	1.00

64 Squadron

21/09/43	Ferraby	Mitchell Escort	0850–1025	1.35
23/09/43	Ferraby	Mitchell Escort	0735–0905	1.30
24/09/43	Harder	Marauder Escort	1045–1235	1.50
27/09/43	Calder	B-17 Escort	1045–1200	1.15
29/09/43	Calder	Shipping Recce	1045–1220	1.35
02/10/43	Harder	Jim Crow	0700–0840	1.40
03/10/43	Harder	Marauder Escort	1035–1215	1.40
06/10/43	Harder	Convoy Patrol	1415–1600	1.45
18/10/43	Harder	Marauder Escort	0825–1025	2.00
19/10/43	Bilsland	Beaufighter Escort	1025–1200	1.35
23/10/43	Harder	Beaufighter Escort	1110–1245	1.35
24/10/43	Harder	Mitchell Escort	1550–1745	1.55
03/11/43	Harder	Marauder Escort	1445–1645	2.00
25/11/43	Ormerod	Shipping Recce	0825–0945	1.20
04/12/43	Swadling	Jim Crow	0845–1030	1.45
04/12/43	Duncan	Sweep	1355–1530	1.35

05/12/43	Muzard	Sweep	1320–1500	1.40
13/12/43	Duncan	Marauder Escort	1400–1610	2.10
20/12/43	Duncan	Scramble	0905–1040	1.35
20/12/43	Duncan	B-17 Escort	1205–1415	2.10
21/12/43	Duncan	Jim Crow	0955–1115	1.20
22/12/43	Duncan	Beaufighter Escort	1310–1440	1.30
23/12/43	Duncan	ASR	1515–1630	1.15
30/12/43	Duncan	Mitchell Escort	1310–1505	1.55
13/01/44	Andrews	Jim Crow	0910–1035	1.25
14/01/44	Duncan	Marauder Escort	1055–1240	1.45
15/02/44	Cooper	Shipping Recce	1425–1550	1.25
07/03/44	Duncan	ASR	1145–1330	1.45
07/03/44	Morrison	ASR	1640–1800	1.20
09/03/44	de Verteuil	Shipping Recce (scrubbed)	1050–1115	0.25
15/03/44	Cooper	Jim Crow	0800–0940	1.40
18/03/44	Morrison	ASR	1750–1910	1.20
13/04/44	Morrison	Beaufighter Escort	1450–1645	1.55
18/04/44	Smart	ASR	1725–1945	2.20
23/04/44	Duncan	Jim Crow	1955–2130	2.35
27/04/44	Duncan	Scramble	1935–1950	0.15
02/05/44	Duncan	Marauder Escort	1515–1735	2.20
03/05/44	de Verteuil	Escort-Fabius Exercise	2100–2240	1.40
04/05/44	de Verteuil	Escort-Fabius Exercise	0500–0700	2.00
04/05/44	Morrison	Escort-Fabius Exercise	1015–1205	1.50
05/05/44	Cooper	Escort-Fabius Exercise	0500–0655	1.55
06/05/44	Duncan	Sweep	0815–0955	1.40
08/05/44	Duncan	Sweep	1810–1950	1.40
09/05/44	Maunders	Sweep	0955–1125	1.30
11/05/44	Cooper	Boston Escort	1010–1150	1.40
11/05/44	Cooper	Sweep	1600–1750	1.50
12/05/44	Duncan	Bomber Escort/Sweep	1030–1150	1.20
12/05/44	Duncan	Marauder Support Cover	1835–2000	1.25
13/05/44	Smiley	Mitchell Escort	1010–1140	1.30
13/05/44	de Verteuil	Boston Escort	1520 -1700	1.40
15/05/44	Smiley	Shipping Recce	2100–2225	1.25
18/05/44	Duncan	Patrol	2100–2200	1.00
19/05/44	Morrison	Sweep	1930–2045	1.15
21/05/44	Thorpe	Sweep	0720–0840	1.20
23/05/44	Duncan	Mitchell Escort	1615–1815	2.00
24/05/44	Coupar	Boston Escort	1015–1150	1.35
24/05/44	Duncan	Mitchell Escort	1830–2025	1.55
25/05/44	Maunders	Scramble	0450–0550	1.00
27/05/44	Duncan	Bomber Escort	1110–1240	1.30

27/05/44	Travis	Bomber Escort/Sweep	1820 2020	2.00
28/05/44	Duncan	Boston Escort	1205–1335	1.30
29/05/44	Duncan	Mitchell Escort	1500–1715	2.15
30/05/44	Andrews	Mitchell Escort	1035–1225	1.50
24/06/44	Williams	Convoy Patrol	1510–1640	1.30
27/06/44	Smart	Convoy Patrol	0825–1020	1.55
27/06/44	Meharry	Typhoon Escort/Sweep	1250–1445	1.55

611 Squadron

04/07/44	Walker	Shipping Recce	0950–1110	1.20
07/07/44	Walker	Sweep	1805–2020	2.15
09/07/44	Walker	Shipping Recce	1955–2130	1.35
11/07/44	McNeil	Rhubarb	1405–1605	2.00

234 Squadron

19/07/44	May	Sweep	1455–1605	1.10
19/07/44	Morgan	Shipping Recce	2110–2245	1.35
22/07/44	May	Shipping Recce	0625–0800	1.35
22/07/44	Farmiloe	Mosquito Escort	1915–2005	0.50
23/07/44	May	Shipping Recce	2005–2245	2.40
24/07/44	May	Naval Escort	2050–2230	1.40
25/07/44	Farmiloe	Rhubarb	1400–1535	1.35
27/07/44	Butler	Rhubarb	1900–2050	1.50
28/07/44	Butler	Shipping Recce	0905–1035	1.30
31/07/44	May	Shipping Recce	2110–2230	1.20
01/08/44	Farmiloe	Scramble	0905–1025	1.20
05/08/44	Stebbings	Shipping Recce	0615–0815	2.00
05/08/44	Berry	Special Ops Escort	2050–2305	2.15
06/08/44	Berry	Shipping Recce	1510–1640	1.30
06/08/44	Berry	Shipping Recce	1720–1820	1.00
11/08/44	May	Mosquito Escort	1800–2000	2.00
13/08/44	Farmiloe	Sweep	1950–2200	2.10
14/08/44	Halloran	Rhubarb	1240–1400	1.20
20/08/44	Farmiloe	VIP Escort	0645–0845	2.00
30/08/44	Morgan	Rhubarb	1750–1950	2.00
01/09/44	Morgan	Armed Recce	0705–0915	2.10
01/09/44	Crowhurst	Armed Recce	1145–1340	1.55
01/09/44	Morgan	Mitchell Escort	1945–2105	1.20
03/09/44	Crowhurst	Marauder Escort	1705–1815	1.10
05/09/44	Harry	Armed Recce	1650–1910	2.20
06/09/44	Stebbings	Weather Recce	0650–0930	2.40
09/09/44	May	Armed Recce	1250–1505	2.15
10/09/44	Morgan	Armed Recce	1305–1530	2.25
11/09/44	May	Naval Escort	1100–1350	2.50
11/09/44	Morgan	Naval Escort	1715–1750	0.35
12/09/44	Farmiloe	VIP Escort	0945–1205	2.20
12/09/44	Farmiloe	VIP Escort	1530–1650	1.20

14/09/44	Morgan	Halifax Escort	1120–1340	2.20
14/09/44	Fargher	Halifax Escort	1515–1735	2.20
15/09/44	Morgan	Armed Recce	1520–1750	2.30
17/09/44	May	Escort Airborne Forces	1220–1445	2.25
18/09/44	Fargher	Escort Anti Flak Patrol	1330–1555	2.25
19/09/44	May	Escort Airborne Forces	1410–1620	2.10
20/09/44	Halloran	Escort Anti Flak Patrol	1735–1905	1.30
23/09/44	May	Escort Airborne Forces	1635–1915	2.40
26/09/44	May	Mitchell Escort	0920–1100	1.40

63 Squadron

12/10/44	Scholey	Lancaster Escort	0715–0920	2.05
28/10/44	Scholey	Halifax/Lancaster Escort	0915–1105	1.50

Summary

Squadron	Operations	Hours
92	52	71.00
54	5	5.35
118	42	65.00
64	66	108.15
611	4	7.10
234	41	76.40
63	2	3.55
Total	212	337.35

Appendix E

Non-operational Flying

The following information has been taken from pilots' logbooks and is intended to give an insight into the type of non-operational flying that the Darlington Spitfire carried out during its service career.

Date	Pilot	Squadron	Detail	Duration
20/07/41	Kingaby	92	air test and air firing	0.30
21/07/41	Kingaby	92	West Malling–Biggin	0.15
04/08/41	Kingaby	92	local flying	0.20
09/08/41	Kingaby	92	air test	0.20
20/08/41	Kingaby	92	weather test	0.05
27/08/41	Kingaby	92	local flying	0.40
28/08/41	Kingaby	92	local flying	0.20
07/09/41	Kingaby	92	local flying	0.10
07/09/41	Kingaby	92	local flying	0.40
12/09/41	Kingaby	92	air test	0.35
13/09/41	Kingaby	92	formation practice	0.20
13/09/41	Kingaby	92	formation practice	0.25
14/09/41	Kingaby	92	weather test	0.10
16/09/41	Kingaby	92	local flying	0.30
22/09/41	Kingaby	92	local flying	0.30
22/09/41	Kingaby	92	local flying	0.15
25/09/41	Kingaby	92	Biggin Hill–Gravesend	0.20
26/09/41	Kingaby	92	local flying	0.15
30/09/41	Kingaby	92	Gravesend–Biggin Hill	0.20
30/09/41	Kingaby	92	Biggin Hill–Gravesend	0.15
02/10/41	Kingaby	92	local flying	0.40
02/10/41	Kingaby	92	to Biggin (conference)	0.15
04/10/41	Kingaby	92	air test	0.10
10/10/41	Kingaby	92	air test	0.15
13/10/41	Kingaby	92	local flying	0.20
13/10/41	Kingaby	92	to Biggin Hill	0.15
16/10/41	Kingaby	92	Manston–Gravesend	0.20
16/10/41	Kingaby	92	local flying	0.20
04/08/43	Harbison	118	formation/cine gun	0.40
23/08/43	Harbison	118	cannon test	0.25
04/09/43	Harbison	118	to Coltishall for ops	0.55
04/09/43	Harbison	118	from Coltishall (recalled)	0.50

14/03/44	Cooper	64	practice bombing	1.05
16/03/44	Cooper	64	formation practice	1.00
07/04/44	Morrison	64	formation practice	0.20
11/04/44	Cooper	64	practice bombing	1.05
13/04/44	Cooper	64	practice bombing	1.15
13/04/44	Morrison	64	night formation	1.15
11/05/44	Cooper	64	to Manston for ops	0.25
11/05/44	Cooper	64	to Hawkinge for ops	0.20
03/07/44	Walker	611	Harrowbeer–Predannack	0.30
09/07/44	Walker	611	cine gun	0.40
28/07/44	Halloran	234	cine gun	0.50
05/08/44	Stebbings	234	Bolt Head–Predannack	0.25
09/08/44	Farmiloe	234	formation practice	1.00
11/08/44	May	234	to Manston for ops	1.45
12/08/44	May	234	from Manston ex ops	1.45
13/08/44	Stebbings	234	practice bombing	0.40
14/08/44	Halloran	234	to Tangmere for ops	1.00
14/08/44	Halloran	234	from Tangmere ex ops	1.15
16/08/44	May	234	formation practice	0.35
17/08/44	Stebbings	234	cine gun	0.40
23/08/44	Farmiloe	234	cannon and u/c test	0.15
27/08/44	Halloran	234	air test	0.10
28/08/44	May	234	to North Weald	1.30
05/09/44	Halloran	234	cannon test	0.35
06/09/44	Stebbings	234	Manston–North Weald	0.45
12/09/44	Farmiloe	234	to Hendon	0.15
13/09/44	Farmiloe	234	Amiens–North Weald	1.30
13/09/44	May	234	cannon test	1.20
28/09/44	Farmiloe	234	cine gun / formation	1.00

North Star

The £5000 donated by the Chairman and Managing Director of Henry Williams Ltd led to the naming of Darlington's second Spitfire which emerged from the shadow aircraft factory at Castle Bromwich in October 1941. It too was a Mark Vb, serial number AD387, and bore the inscription *North Star*, a famous name in railway history dating back to an engine designed and built in 1830 by Robert Stephenson for the Stockton and Darlington Railway. Unlike the baptism of fire experienced by the Darlington Spitfire, AD387 was to have a leisurely introduction to active service courtesy of the Poles of 316 Squadron who were based at Church Stanton in Somerset, an airfield that was occasionally referred to as Tricky Warren, the quaintly rural name of a local village.

Number 316 Squadron was tasked with the defence of Bristol and Exeter, but the German invasion of Russia led to a marked scaling down of operations over the west country, and by late 1941 most of their flying was non-operational. *North Star*'s first sortie took place on 19 November when Flight Lieutenant Alexander Gabszewicz carried out cannon tests, followed by a local flight to Exeter. Although it was to be mainly engaged on training sorties, it did occasionally venture over to France and on 25 November it was flown by Battle of Britain ace Flight Lieutenant Tadeusz Nowierski DFC on a weather reconnaissance. Three days later he flew it again during a sector recce, but neither operation produced any reaction from the Germans.

On 12 December 1941, 316 Squadron moved to Northolt to join 11 Group, but AD387 was left behind for the incoming Poles of 306 Squadron. Its fortunes were not to change a great deal with its new unit and in the early months of 1942 it continued to lead a relatively quiet life. Following a move to Kirton-in-Lindsey in Lincolnshire, it underwent a major inspection at General Aircraft Ltd before being issued to 12 MU at Kirkbride on 8 November 1942 where it joined up with W3320. Whereas the Darlington Spitfire was destined to remain with the RAF as a low-altitude fighter, AD387 was about to have a complete change of scene and on 14 March 1943, it was delivered to Air Service Training at Hamble for conversion to a Seafire Ib for use by the Fleet Air Arm.

At the start of the war the elements that together formed Britain's air power varied greatly in the quality of their equipment. One of the poor relations was the Fleet Air Arm which entered the war with a number of types that were obsolete when compared with their land based equivalent. Even by 1942 the situation had not improved a great deal and the Navy was still desperately short of effective fighters. To try to improve their plight in the short term, a number of ex-RAF Spitfire Mark Vs, including AD387, were navalised, the major modification being the fitting of an A-frame arrester hook, together with strengthening of the rear fuselage to cater for the increased loadings. As the aircraft were wanted quickly, no wing folding mechanism was incorporated, and the only other modification of any significance was the provision of slinging points fore and aft of the cockpit.

By early May, work on AD387 had been completed and the aircraft, now wearing its Navy serial number NX899, was delivered to RNAS Stretton in Cheshire on the 14th. Sadly the Navy were not as co-operative as the RAF with regard to the inscriptions of presentation aircraft and it appears that the name *North Star* did not feature on the aircraft after its conversion.

It first served with 809 Squadron, but in true Navy tradition it was not long before it was in the wars when hydraulic failure caused its undercarriage to collapse on landing on 29 June. It was then transferred to 801 Squadron where it was coded 'U' but suffered another accident on 4 November when a heavy landing on the deck of HMS *Furious* resulted in the starboard undercarriage leg being forced up through the wing.

There were to be further traumas on 2 February 1944 during deck landing trials on HMS *Furious* when the port undercarriage leg would not lower and a wheels up landing had to be made at RNAS Hatston in the Orkney Islands.

On 11 February NX899 had it greatest day when it saw action off the Norwegian coast. Together with two battleships, two cruisers and seven destroyers, HMS *Furious* had sailed from Scapa Flow on the 9th with a strike force of twelve Barracudas who were to operate against German shipping in the area. During the course of the day the Seafires were involved in a number of skirmishes with defending *Luftwaffe* fighters and although one Seafire was lost, this was avenged by NX899's pilot, Sub-Lieutenant L.D. Wilkinson, who shot down a Messerschmitt Me 109G near Stadlandet and damaged two others. The primary target of the Barracudas was the 5000 ton German merchant vessel *Ensland* which was located and sunk near Vaagso.

In August 1944 NX899 was passed to 759 Squadron at Yeovilton but was to suffer a further mishap on 5 September when it ended up on its nose after a tyre burst on landing. Later in the year it was transferred to 761 Squadron at Henstridge but it disappears from the records in December 1944 and, like the Darlington Spitfire, its eventual fate is not known.

Bibliography

Andrews, C.F. & Morgan, E.B. (1981) *Supermarine Aircraft Since 1914*. Putnam.

Bowyer, C. (1984) *Fighter Pilots of the RAF 1939–45*. William Kimber.

Bowyer, M.J.F. (1992) *2 Group RAF*. Crecy Books.

Franks, N. (1994) *Sky Tiger*. Crecy Books.

Franks, N. (1995) (Ed.) *Neville Duke War Diaries*. Grub Street.

Freeman, R.A. (1970) *The Mighty Eighth*. MacDonald and Janes.

Lucas, P.B. & Johnson, J.E. (1995) *Winged Victory*. Stanley Paul.

Middlebrook, M. & Everett, C. (1985) *Bomber Command War Diaries*. Viking.

Morgan, E.B. & Shacklady, E. (1987) *Spitfire – The History*. Key Publishing.

Price, A. (1982) *The Spitfire Story*. Arms and Armour.

Ogley, R. (1990) *Biggin On the Bump*. Froglet.

Rawlings, J.D.R. (1969) *Fighter Squadrons of the RAF*. MacDonald and Janes.

Sturtivant, R. & Burrow, M. (1995) *Fleet Air Arm Aircraft 1939 to 1945*. Air Britain.

Shores, C., Cull, B. & Malizia, N. (1991) *Malta, The Spitfire Year – 1942*. Grub Street.

Shores, C. & Williams, C. (1994) *Aces High*. Grub Street.

Smith, C. (1992) *The History of the Glider Pilot Regiment*. Leo Cooper.

Action Stations, Volumes 1–10. PSL.

Index

Names (Ranks as contemporary)

Anderton, C. F/Sgt 53
Andrews, E. F/L 75–6, 85–7, 90, 92–3, 121–2
Arnott, P.L. S/L 100–1
Atkins, Sgt 40

Bader, D.R.S. S/L 51
Baldwin, J.R. G/C 139
Beake, P.H. P/O 23–5, 123–4
Bernard, M. Lt 84, 89–90, 102
Berry, T.W. F/L 105, 111
Beurling, G. P/O 133
Bilsland, W. F/O 70, 72
Blatchford, H.P. W/C 51
Brettell, G.E. P/O 27–9, 34, 124–5
Brown, F.T. F/O 55–6
Bruce, E.A.G.C. P/O 27, 34, 39
Buglass, E.A. P/O 58
Butler, A.C. F/Sgt 103

Calder, K.V. F/O 69
Carpenter, Sgt 31
Cassidy, E. S/L 71, 73, 76
Chapman, S/L 76
Clostermann, P. Sgt 142
Collard, H.W. P/O 128
Collishaw, R. AVM 45
Cooper, A.G.H. F/L 71–2, 74, 76, 78–80, 82, 86–9, 94, 125–7
Coupar, G.C. P/O 156
Cox, H. Sgt 36, 38–9
Crowhurst, J.W.C. F/Sgt 110
de la Torre, S/L 38
de Verteuil, N.J. P/O 67, 76–7, 80, 82, 91
Donaldson, A. W/C 133

Douglas, W.A. S/L 98
Drew, A. F/L 63–4
Duke, N.F. P/O 20, 24, 27, 32–4
Duncan, J.D.M. F/Sgt 73, 75, 77, 80, 82, 91–2, 127–9
Dunning, P.S. F/O 59–61

Fargher, T.P. F/Sgt 101, 113, 129–31
Farmiloe, S.T. F/Sgt 87–8, 101–04, 111, 113, 131–2
Farquharson, G.H.T. F/Sgt 44, 132–3
Ferguson, D. F/O 108
Ferraby, D.L. F/O 66, 133–4
Flight, R.J. P/O 51–64, 134–7
Freeborn, J.C. S/L 51, 57

Gabszewicz, A.K. F/L 166
Gibbs, E.M. F/L 44, 137–8
Goodman, G.H. W/C 105
Grant, S.B. S/L 133
Gwynne, W. Sgt 44

Halloran, S.C. P/O 105–6
Harbison, W. P/O 64, 138–9
Harder, J.W. F/O 67–72, 75–6, 78–9, 84, 89, 139–41
Harrison, S. Sgt 21, 29
Harry, R.H. F/O 110
Hartley, P.W. S/L 45
Hickman, G.P. Sgt 23, 29–30
Hogan, H.A.V. W/C 124
Hollingworth, J. Sgt 58–9
Humphreys, P. F/O 21

Johnston, W.L.H. Sgt 21–4, 29, 31, 36–40, 100, 105, 109, 129, 141–3
Jones, F.E. Sgt 41
Jones, J. Sgt 59

Kelly, F/O 73
Kingaby, D.E. F/Sgt 20–3, 25–7, 30–40, 90, 143–5
Lattimer, C.H. F/L 100
Law, F/O 78
Leigh-Mallory, ACM Sir T. 129–30
Le Peutrec, M. Sgt 45
Liby, S.K. 2nd Lt 60
Lucas, P.B. W/C 51, 57, 69, 71
Lund, J.W. F/L 24–5, 34
Lyon, E.R. F/O 103

MacDonald, N.G. F/Sgt 99
Mack, K. F/Sgt 152
MacKenzie, J. S/L 78–9, 96
Malan, A.G. W/C 20, 22, 24, 29, 34, 100, 144
Marcinkus, R. F/L 125
Maunders, G.R. F/Sgt 77–8, 85
May, J.R. P/O 101, 107, 111–13, 145–7
McNeil, D.L. W/O 99
Meharry, H.J. F/O 93–4
Metcalfe, J. F/Sgt 102
Milne, R.M. S/L 29, 39
Morgan, A. F/Sgt 109–10, 112
Morrison, W.S. F/Sgt 80, 83, 91, 147–9
Muzard, J. Lt 73

Newbery, R.A. F/L 53, 55, 135
Nikl, V. F/Sgt 118
Nowierski, T. F/L 166

Ormerod, J.B. F/O 71

Painter, W. F/O 129, 142
Paull, N.K. F/Sgt 52
Phillips, E.W.H. P/O 25
Picard, H. F/L 125
Pickering, George 19
Pickering, J. F/L 50
Plagis, J. F/L 66–7, 72
Powell, W/C 85

Rankin, J. S/L 20, 29
Reveilhac, P/O 44
Robinson, M. S/L 29

Sanderson, J.H. F/L 145
Scholey, J.D. F/L 117–18
Shepherd, J.B. F/L 53
Smallbone, D. W/O 64
Smart, W.A. F/O 90–1, 95–6
Smiley, D.A.B. F/O 71, 82
Soden, G/C 28
Spencer, F.L. Sgt 63
Stebbings, R.D. F/L 104, 107, 110, 149–50
Swadling, F. F/Sgt 72

Talalla, C.L.F. F/O 52, 57
Thorne, Sgt 73
Thorpe, A.T. F/O 77, 83
Travis, A. F/Sgt 84
Trent, L. S/L 51

Varney, Sgt 44
Vinter, S.H. Sgt 24

Walenn, G. F/L 125
Walker, I.G. F/Sgt 87, 96–8, 152–3
Walton, W.C. F/L 100, 103
Watson, S.K. F/O 54–6
Wawn, Sgt 27
Wheeler, N. W/C 68
Wilkinson, L.D. Sub/Lt 167
Williams, R.A.L. F/Sgt 92
Woods-Scawen, Sgt 36, 38

Airfields (UK)
Acaster Malbis 123
Acklington 139
Aston Down 127
Ayr 66, 76, 126
Biggin Hill 20–31, 35, 38, 100, 122
Bolt Head 80
Boxted 60
Bradwell Bay 73, 75, 122
Burnaston 135
Calveley 134
Cambridge 145
Castle Bromwich 43
Castletown 43–6, 65, 121
Catfoss 127, 144
Catterick 43

Index

Charmy Down 51
Chipping Norton 123
Church Stanton 166
Coltishall 50–60, 68–79
Cosford 19
Cranfield 50

Deanland 80–92
Debden 143
Digby 39, 41

Eastleigh 19
Elgin 121
Eshott 96, 134, 150

Filton 50
Friston 68

Grangemouth 27, 123–4
Gravesend 30–42

Hamble 42, 166
Harrowbeer 92–6
Hatfield 124, 138
Hatston 167
Hawarden 123, 134
Hendon 111
Henstridge 167
Hornchurch 24, 123
Horsham St Faith 137–8
Hullavington 125, 127

Kenley 59
Kirkbride 46–8, 166
Kirton-in-Lindsey 127, 145, 147, 166

Leconfield 123
Leeming 139
Lee on Solent 117
Leuchars 139
Llandow 41
Longtown 46
Luton 125

Manston 38–9, 73, 75, 82–3, 105, 110, 143
Martlesham Heath 60
Matlaske 58
Merston 61–4

Middleton St George 128, 139
Milfield 124, 133, 140
Molesworth 74
Montrose 134

Newton 134
North Coates 68
North Weald 107–19

Pembrey 47
Peterborough 125, 150
Peterhead 64
Portreath 141
Predannack 96–107

Rednal 126, 128, 135

Sealand 124
Skaebrae 152
Stretton 167
Sumburgh 121, 152
Sutton Bridge 100, 142

Tangmere 59, 69, 80, 105
Tern Hill 135, 147
Thornaby 137
Thorney Island 123
Turnhouse 123

Upavon 125, 142

Warmwell 100, 141
Watton 128, 145
Westhampnett 60–1
West Malling 65–8
Whitchurch 123
Wittering 21

Yeovilton 167

Airfields (overseas)
Australia Darwin 137–8
Canada Aylmer 128
         Kingston 125, 135
         Neepawa 128
Egypt Bilbeis 143
        Heliopolis 66
France Coulombs (B6) 129
         Martragny (B7) 124
         Sommervieu (B8) 123
Germany Wildenrath 139

Airfields (overseas) (*cont.*)
Korea   Kimpo 139
Malta   Luqa 122
           Takali 134
Rhodesia Belvedere 145
           Cranbourne 145
USA   March AFB 138

Airfields (*Luftwaffe*)
Abbeville 34
Beaumont le Roger 60, 62, 64
Beauvais 105
Calais Marck 22
Evreux 62, 67, 70, 82
Kerlin Bastard 98, 103
Le Touquet 26–7, 73
Lille-Vendeville 82
Monchy Breton 62
Merville 63
Poix-Nord 60
Schiphol 57, 59, 71, 73
St Omer 25, 59, 61
Vannes 98
Vitry-en-Artois 61
Woensdrecht 60

RAF squadrons
5   131
17   121
23   139
24   111
29   139
54   43–6, 137–8
63   117–19
64   62, 65–96, 122–3, 126–9, 138,
       140, 143, 147–8
67   139
72   26, 29, 35, 41, 145
74   139
92   19–30, 31–42, 141
107   25, 59, 62
111   143
118   50–65, 135–6, 138
122   143
126   132
133   124

134   45
141   70
143   53
151   101, 105
152   21, 141
154   122
164   123
180   57
185   133
192   112
193   123
229   122
234   80, 87–90, 99–116, 129–32,
       145–7
242   51
249   41, 51, 133
257   138
263   93, 138
278   79
298   104
306   166
310   118
313   118
316   166
342   62
350   90
402   53, 57, 71
416   53, 57, 70–1, 133
452   137
457   137
487   51
511   132
601   123
603   16
608   137
609   26, 29, 35–6
611   34, 57, 59, 70–1, 75, 79–80, 87,
       97–9, 152–3
616   63
644   104
695   137

RAF – other units
22 AACU 134
14 APC 76

Index

1524 BAT Flight 134
2 CTW 129, 131
1330 CU 143
1 EFTS 124, 138
22 EFTS 145
29 E&RTFS 125
30 EFTS 135
35 EFTS 128
2 FIS 134
16 FPP 47
7 OTU 123
41 OTU 119, 134
53 OTU 41, 127, 145, 147
56 OTU 137
57 OTU 96, 150
58 OTU 27, 123–4, 140
61 OTU 100, 126, 128, 133, 135, 142
226 OCU 139
228 OCU 139
12 MU 46–7, 166
24 MU 42
56 MU 46
5(P)AFU 135, 137, 147
7(P)AFU 150
11(P)AFU 134
17(P)AFU 128, 145
5 SFTS 124
7 SFTS 125
9 SFTS 125
14 SFTS 128
15 SFTS 123
20 SFTS 145
31 SFTS 125, 135
3501 SU 50
2 TAF 131, 139
CFE 138
CFS 127, 142
CGS 100, 142
FLS 51, 124, 127, 140
1 Group 117
4 Group 118

FAA – squadrons
759 167
761 167

801 167
809 167

USAAF units
303 BG 74
322 BG 58
386 BG 60
1 FG 138
335 TFS 138

Luftwaffe **units**
JG 53 16
KG 26 9
KG 51 77
ZG 76 9

RAF aircraft – Spitfire
P8644 44
R6919 25
R7122 120
R7132 120
W3179 30
W3314 22, 121
W3315 120
W3324 23
W3381 24
W3822 145
W3895 36
X4257 95–6
AB500 134
AD125 32, 40
AD387/NX899 12, 47, 166–7
AD453 44
AD565 78
AR292 77
AR343 103
AR433 63
AR447 58
AR450 57
AR453 64
AR549 70
BL232 118
BL415 44, 143
BL472 70
BL646 84
BL734 67, 78
BL810 112

RAF aircraft – Spitfire (*cont.*)
BM200 103
BR176 132
BR294 133
BS164 138
BS282 152
EN966 55
EP191 58
EP413 51, 135
EP549 53
MA228 118
MJ787 133
MK258 140
MK805 127

Hurricane
BM964 122

Mustang
FB152 130

FB215 146
FB222 150
KH721 122
KH743 152

Liberator
AL516 132

Beaufighter
EL240 53
JL890 53

Mitchell
FL164 71
FL683 67
FV944 67

Dakota
FD797 111

Typhoon
DN432 123